THE BOOK *of* ENOCH *for* BEGINNERS

THE BOOK *of*
ENOCH
for BEGINNERS

A Guide to Expand Your
Understanding of the Biblical World

PHILLIP J. LONG

**ROCKRIDGE
PRESS**

First Rockridge Press trade paperback edition 2022

Rockridge Press and the Rockridge Press logo are trademarks or registered trademarks of Callisto Media Inc. and/or its affiliates in the United States and other countries and may not be used without written permission.

For general information on our other products and services, please contact our Customer Care Department within the United States at (866) 744-2665, or outside the United States at (510) 253-0500.

Paperback ISBN: 978-1-68539-645-9 | eBook ISBN: 978-1-68539-816-3

Manufactured in the United States of America

Interior and Cover Designer: Monica Cheng
Art Producer: Maya Melenchuk
Editor: Adrian Potts
Production Editor: Ellina Litmanovich
Production Manager: Martin Worthington

All images used under license © Dandylyon Designs/ Creative Market and Shutterstock.

10 9 8 7 6 5 4 3 2 1 0

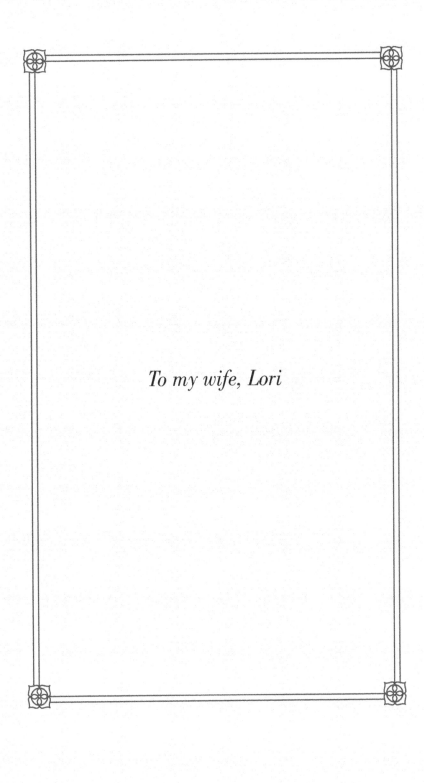

To my wife, Lori

CONTENTS

INTRODUCTION

—

Books like 1 Enoch have fascinated me since high school. I found a used copy of *The Lost Books of the Bible* in a bargain bin at a used bookstore, and, even though I grew up in a Christian community, this was the first time I heard these books existed. To be honest, reading these "hidden" books felt rebellious!

Much later, in my first PhD seminar, I read through the entire Old Testament pseudepigrapha and wrote a lengthy paper on the value of each of these books for the study of early Judaism and the New Testament. I often returned to 1 Enoch as part of my dissertation research. I have since integrated much of my research into undergraduate classes on apocalyptic literature and early Judaism. In 2016, I edited some of that research and published it on my blog, ReadingActs.com. These posts are among the most popular, attracting readers from all over the world interested in what this unique Jewish apocalyptic book says.

The goal of this book is to help readers make sense of 1 Enoch. This is not a new translation of the book, but a summary and commentary on 1 Enoch designed for the nonspecialist. Some introductions to 1 Enoch focus only on the first thirty-six chapters, which is known as the Book of the

Watchers. This is understandable, since, for many, this is the most interesting section. However, in this book I will look at all five sections of 1 Enoch, since each contributes uniquely to our understanding of early Judaism and Christianity. I want to help readers hear the various voices and set the historical context in a way that sheds light on an obscure book.

As you begin your journey through the strange world of 1 Enoch, I invite you to read the text for yourself and use this book like a tourist guidebook. I will point out key features and how the book sheds light on how some Jewish writers understood their place in their rapidly changing world.

HOW TO
USE THIS BOOK

—

Part 1 is an introduction to who Enoch was and the religious and historical context of 1 Enoch. In part 2, I will guide you through the five major sections—the books within the book. I'll start with an introduction that summarizes what's in that book, then mention a few key facts about the history and content. Then I'll divide each book into sections. Each section will begin with a summary of the narrative, followed by a few key verses. If you're really interested, I recommend finding a full translation of 1 Enoch and reading the complete section, but these key verses will highlight the main ideas. Then I will provide a short commentary on the section, offering historical and theological context and pointing out key features of the section. You will also find boxes that will give you an in-depth look at some interesting features of 1 Enoch. These boxes will explain key figures and biblical connections and occasionally deal with translation issues.

You do not need to read this book in any order nor feel compelled to read it from beginning to end. Like a tourist guidebook, flip to the section that interests you at the moment! You may decide to read a section in 1 Enoch, then flip to the corresponding section of this book to read my explanation.

PART ONE

AN INTRODUCTION
to 1 ENOCH

1 Enoch is a misunderstood book in popular media. You may have watched videos on YouTube claiming that it was suppressed in the early church because it disagreed with mainstream Christianity. Darren Aronofsky's 2014 film *Noah* was loosely based on the Book of the Watchers. 1 Enoch was even mentioned on an episode of *Ancient Aliens*, a documentary series that implied the book was removed from the Bible because it was proof of humanity's extraterrestrial origins. Because of this kind of misinformation, it is important to understand what 1 Enoch says in its true historical and literary context.

1 Enoch is important for the study of early Judaism and Christianity. 1 Enoch is sometimes described as "lost," and the Western Church rarely accepted it as authoritative. Four of the five sections of 1 Enoch appear in the Dead Sea Scrolls, indicating some Jews in the first century valued the book, although it was never considered canonical. The book was virtually unknown outside the Ethiopian Orthodox Church until the nineteenth century.

Yale University professor John Collins suggests that the publication of 1 Enoch in English in the early nineteenth century was the key motivation for biblical scholars to study early Jewish literature. The study of books like 1 Enoch affects the study of the Gospels, Paul, and the Book of Revelation, as well.

Understanding the Book of Enoch

The study of 1 Enoch is important for modern readers for several reasons. First, the book is a pre-Christian apocalypse that was used by early Christians. Jude 14–15 quotes 1 Enoch 1:9 and it is possible 1 Peter 3:19–20 refers to the Book of the Watchers. Since 1 Enoch refers to a "son of man," some Christian scholars suggest a connection to Jesus.

Second, 1 Enoch offers insight into the relatively unknown period of Jewish history before 165 BCE. The Book of the Watchers interprets and develops the Flood story from Genesis and explains how evil entered God's good creation and anticipates God's coming destruction of this world. A section known as The Animal Apocalypse (chapters 85–90) is an allegorical summary of Jewish history up to the Maccabean Revolt (164–160 BCE, against the Seleucid Empire, the descendants of Alexander the Great). The Enoch literature also lays the foundation for medieval Jewish mysticism.

Third, the book's unusual contents have long appeared in literature and popular media. For example, Milton's *Paradise Lost* (1667) may allude to the Enoch legends. The descriptions of heaven, angels, and demons fascinate many readers. Some of the names of angels and demons from 1 Enoch appear on popular TV shows such as *Supernatural*. Others use the book to support conspiracy theories about a flat Earth and alien abductions.

There are two other books associated with Enoch. 2 Enoch is a Jewish document written in the late first century CE known primarily from a Slavic translation. 3 Enoch is a Jewish mystical book that claims to be written by Rabbi Ishmael (a great sage from Galilee who lived from 90 to 135 CE), although most scholars date the book to the fifth or sixth century. Both books include descriptions of heavenly journeys, the punishment of the wicked, and fantastic angels.

The Books within the Book

The title *1 Enoch* was not used in the ancient world. What we call 1 Enoch today is a compilation of at least five books written as early as the third century BCE in Judea. Complete versions existed only in Ethiopic (a language also known as Ge'ez) manuscripts dating to the sixteenth century.

Book 1: The Book of the Watchers (chapters 1–36) was written in the late third century BCE. It expands on Genesis 6:1–4, which mentions the "sons of God" who took human wives and the mysterious Nephilim. This section explains why God destroyed the world in the Flood and describes Enoch's heavenly journeys.

Book 2: The Book of Parables (chapters 37–71) was written after 40 BCE. Enoch's parables report what he saw on his heavenly journeys. Since this section describes an apocalyptic judgment and the coming of the chosen one, it is of special interest to Christians.

Book 3: The Book of Astronomical Writings (chapters 72–82) is the oldest section of 1 Enoch, written as early as the third century BCE. It argues for a 365-day solar calendar as opposed to the lunar calendar that was in use by most Jews at the time. Although this may seem strange to modern readers, using the right calendar was important in first-century Judaism. If someone used the wrong calendar, they might unknowingly profane the Sabbath or the Day of Atonement.

Book 4: The Book of Dream Visions (chapters 83–90) was written after 164–160 BCE. The first dream predicts the coming flood and a future final judgment. The second dream is a complicated allegory of Israel's history known as the Animal Apocalypse.

Book 5: The Epistle of Enoch (chapters 91–108) contains several separate works and forms a conclusion to the collection. The Testimony of Enoch is Enoch's last words to his son Methuselah. The Epistle of Enoch describes a coming final judgment. The Epistle also includes the Apocalypse of Weeks, an apocalyptic summary of human history as ten periods that culminate in the judgment of the watchers and the appearance of the new heavens.

How Enoch Was Rediscovered

Although ancient Christian and Jewish writers refer to 1 Enoch, European scholars knew little about the book; fragments existed, but the only complete copy was thought to be lost in Ethiopia. But in 1773 Scottish lord and adventurer James Bruce was on a quest to find the source of the Blue Nile and came upon the book, written in Ge'ez, in Abyssinia (modern Ethiopia). He brought home three complete copies.

Bruce gave one copy to Louis XV, the king of France, and another to the Bodleian Library at Oxford University. Oxford scholar Richard Laurence translated this manuscript into English in 1821. (This book uses the 1913 translation by Irish Anglican theologian R. H. Charles.)

Fragments of the book have been published in Latin, Greek, Aramaic (the common language of the ancient Near East), Syriac (a dialect of Aramaic used in Syria), and Coptic (the language of Egyptian Christianity). The oldest fragments are Aramaic portions of four sections found among the Dead Sea Scrolls; they were not published until 1978. There are translations available on the Internet, but the translators did not have access to recently published manuscripts and often translate the book in a formal style that's hard to read.

IS 1 ENOCH PART of the BIBLE?

Before beginning a study of 1 Enoch, it is important to understand some key concepts. The book is noncanonical, which means it was never accepted as authoritative by the Jews or by most Christians, and is not considered part of the Bible.

It is also not part of the Apocrypha—a collection of Jewish books written between the Old and New Testaments. The Apocryphal books include Maccabees and Sirach. These books are not part of the Jewish canon, either. Although not authoritative, they were considered valuable by many Jews and Christians and were eventually accepted as canonical by the Roman Catholic Church in 1546 at the Council of Trent.

1 Enoch belongs to a different collection, known as the pseudepigrapha (false writings). This is an unofficial collection of noncanonical Jewish and Christian books, such 4 Ezra, written near the end of the first century CE. This literature is often written in the voice of an ancient prophet to give authority to the text. Among Christians, only the Ethiopian and Eritrean Orthodox Churches use the book as scripture.

1 Enoch is often described as apocalyptic literature. Ancient apocalyptic literature responded to a rapidly changing world by describing current events through the lens of biblical history. Biblical books like Daniel and Revelation used spectacular imagery to cope with persecution and offer hope for the future. 1 Enoch often retells biblical stories to explain the presence of evil in the world and explain the delayed justice of God. In 1 Enoch, although the righteous elect struggle in the present evil age, God will soon judge the world and reward the righteous who remain faithful until the end.

Enoch in Judaism, Islam, and Christianity

Jewish, Christian, and Muslim sacred texts all mention
Enoch. In the Old Testament, the only reference to Enoch is in
Genesis 5:18–24: Enoch "walked with God and was not, for God
took him." There is no explanation for what "God took him"
means, although some have assumed it means that he, like the
prophet Elijah, ascended to heaven. The Jewish philosopher
Philo of Alexandria of the first century CE suggested Enoch was
taken by God because he repented from his wickedness.

In the Quran (19.56–57), Enoch is called Idris and is "a man
of truth (and sincerity), (and) a prophet" and Allah "raised him
to an exalted place."

In the New Testament, Enoch is a model of faithfulness and
a prophet. Enoch is listed in Hebrews 11:5 as a great man of
faith "who did not see death because God took him." This verse
also says Enoch was "commended as having pleased God."
Jude 14 quotes 1 Enoch 1:9, in which Enoch prophesied "the
Lord comes with ten thousand of his holy ones."

Some Christians believe one of the two witnesses that
Revelation (chapter 11) says will return in the last days is Enoch
(the other is Elijah). According to that belief, these two Old
Testament prophets did not die, but ascended to heaven, and
so will come back in the end-times, preach against the kingdom of the beast, be martyred, and then be raised up to heaven
again by God.

1 Enoch 6–36 expands on a few enigmatic verses in
Genesis 6 to explain how evil invaded God's creation. In
Genesis, evil is the result of Adam and Eve's rebellion in Eden;
Christians adopted this view. But in the Book of the Watchers,
Enoch blames evil on rebellious angels who taught humans
to sin. In 1 Enoch, Enoch ascends to heaven, where he sees
the secrets of heaven. He is a "scribe of heaven" who writes
the instructions of the angels. The Jewish book Jubilees from

the first century BCE describes Enoch as the first man to learn writing, study astrology, and create a calendar.

The Enoch literature influenced Jewish and Christian views of reward in heaven and punishment in hell. The book looks forward to a messianic chosen one who will judge the world and inaugurate a temporary messianic kingdom. Enoch's spiritual journeys shape later literary descriptions of heaven and hell, as well. It is even possible that 3 Enoch influenced Dante's *Divine Comedy*.

ENOCH BEYOND the BIBLE

All we know about Enoch from the Old Testament is what the genealogy in Genesis 5 says. He was the father of Methuselah and great-grandfather of Noah. Compared with others in Genesis 5, Enoch's lifespan of 365 years is short (Methuselah lived 969 years).

Enoch is not mentioned in the rest of the Old Testament, but he appears in the Book of Jubilees (another pseudepigraphic book) from the second century BCE. Like 1 Enoch, before the discovery of the Dead Sea Scrolls Jubilees was only known in fifteenth- and sixteenth-century Ethiopic manuscripts. The book summarizes the story of Genesis, relying on what was written in Enoch. Jubilees describes Enoch as the first man who learned to write and interpret the signs of heaven to create a calendar. It says that when Enoch was taken from the world he was led to the Garden of Eden, where he wrote his book condemning the world before the Flood.

In Jewish mystical writings, Enoch becomes an angelic being. In 2 Enoch (written in the late first century CE), he is like an archangel who always stands before God. It also says Enoch wrote 360 books of secret knowledge. In 3 Enoch (written in the fifth century CE), the angel Metatron guides Rabbi Ishmael in his heavenly vision. Although Metatron is known by seventy names, he tells Ishmael he is Enoch, the son of Jared—but is no longer a human. In 3 Enoch 25:2, Enoch/Metatron is described as an otherworldly creature with sixteen faces (four on each side) and one hundred wings on each side. Like the cherubim in Ezekiel, Metatron is covered with eyes: Each of his four sides has 2,190 eyes, for a total of 8,760—the number of hours in a year.

PART TWO

UNCOVERING the FIVE BOOKS of 1 ENOCH

1 Enoch is a collection of at least five books written at different times. Printed editions of these books follow the order of the Ethiopian translation known from sixteenth-century manuscripts, even though this is not the chronological order in which they were written. All five books claim to be the words of Enoch.

In these five books, Enoch is a scribe and prophet who travels to heaven and learns the secrets of the cosmos. As a prophet, he foresees the destruction of the world in the great flood—referring to Noah's time. But the author of 1 Enoch addressed Jewish people living after the late third century BCE who were oppressed by the Greeks and later the Romans. The authors of this literature therefore used a story from their distant past to encourage readers to live righteously in the face of oppression in their own day.

In this part, I will examine each of the five books of 1 Enoch, section by section. I will offer a brief introduction to each of these books, followed by a commentary on the text.

BOOK I

The Book of the Watchers

For many readers, the Book of the Watchers (chapters 1–36) is the most interesting part of 1 Enoch. Written in the third century BCE, the story of fallen angels and the mysterious giants who lived before Noah's flood stir the imagination. This book offers a reason why God destroyed the world with a great flood and explains how evil entered God's good creation. Although this book includes Enoch's prophecy of the coming judgment of the primeval flood, the writer is encouraging readers in his own community, in his own time. Just as God destroyed evil in the past, the book says, he will once again judge those who are oppressing the righteous.

In the first half of the Book of the Watchers, angelic beings known as watchers take human women as wives and have children with them. These children are called the Nephilim (as in Genesis 6:4). In 1 Enoch, the children of the watchers are giants who prey on humans, prompting God to destroy the world with a great flood. Enoch, the seventh generation from Adam and the great-grandfather of Noah, pleads on behalf of the rebellious angels, but God's judgment is settled because they revealed secret, forbidden knowledge to humans.

The second half of the Book of the Watchers is a record of Enoch's journey through the heavens to the ends of the earth. This bizarre journey takes Enoch to the prison where the fallen angels are kept and to the mountain of the dead. He passes through a magnificent garden to Jerusalem, the center of the Earth, where he sees the throne of God. He then travels to the paradise of righteousness, the Garden of Eden.

THE FACTS AT A GLANCE

- The Book of the Watchers was written in the mid to late third century BCE.

- In 1 Enoch, Enoch is a scribe who travels through the heavens and learns secret knowledge. He is a seventh-generation descendant of Adam, father of Methuselah, and great-grandfather of Noah.

- According to Genesis, Enoch did not die. He "walked with God and was no more" (Genesis 5:24).

- According to the Book of the Watchers, rebellious angels taught humans secret knowledge, which led to great evil in the world.

- 1 Enoch contains one of the earliest lists of names for fallen angels and archangels.

- 1 Enoch contains one of the earliest references to a fiery punishment for fallen angels.

- The spirits of the giants destroyed by the great flood become demons.

- During Enoch's heavenly journey, he visits the Garden of Eden and sees the tree Adam and Eve ate from.

Section 1: Chapters 1–5

Like modern books, 1 Enoch begins by establishing the authority of the writer. Most books today print the author's biography and qualifications on the back cover. In 1 Enoch, to confirm Enoch's authority, the author draws a comparison to Moses, the greatest man in biblical history. After drawing attention to their similarities, the writer draws heavily on the Blessing of Moses, in language familiar to readers of Exodus and Deuteronomy, to describe God's coming judgment. "The words of the blessing of Enoch, wherewith he blessed the elect" (1 Enoch 1:1) recalls the final testimony of Moses in Deuteronomy 33:1: "This is the blessing, wherewith Moses the man of God blessed the children of Israel before he died."

There are several themes in chapters 1–5 that will resonate throughout the whole book. First, judgment is coming on the wicked. Like Noah's flood, this judgment is a cataclysm that destroys everything. "The earth shall be wholly rent in sunder, and all that is upon the earth shall perish, and there shall be a judgment upon all" (1:7).

But second, the elect will be preserved from this coming tribulation. In 1 Enoch, the "elect" refers to the writer's righteous community. Like Noah's family, Enoch's community may suffer, but they will ultimately be preserved and vindicated when the final judgment arrives. The righteous will no longer sin and "their lives shall be increased in peace, and the years of their joy shall be multiplied, In eternal gladness and peace, All the days of their life" (5:9).

These are also themes found in biblical apocalyptic texts. Like the Old Testament prophets Isaiah and Micah, Enoch describes God's fiery judgment when he comes with an angelic army. Daniel 12:1–3 says God's people will suffer during a time of great trouble but will be delivered at the final judgment. In the New Testament, Revelation promises final judgment of

God's enemies is coming soon and says God's elect will suffer greatly during a time of persecution but will be vindicated at the final judgment.

KEY VERSE

"And behold! He cometh with ten thousands of His holy ones to execute judgment upon all, and to destroy all the ungodly: and to convict all flesh of all the works of their ungodliness which they have ungodly committed, and of all the hard things which ungodly sinners have spoken against Him."

1 ENOCH 1:9

COMMENTARY

1 Enoch starts by introducing two main characters: Enoch and the watchers. Enoch was a man "whose eyes were opened by God, and saw the vision of the Holy One in the heavens" (1:2). Angels delivered these visions to Enoch, but the visions were for a future generation. Although the coming judgment for Enoch was the Flood, the author is addressing Jewish people living in the third century BCE. The readers of the book are the "future generation" to whom the visions speak.

The term "watchers" describes angelic beings—some of who rebel against God in 1 Enoch 6–11. Not all watchers are rebellious, though; some are called "holy ones." Many of these angelic beings constantly observe the actions of God or are given specific tasks. Daniel 4:13 uses both "watcher" and "holy one" to describe an angel in Nebuchadnezzar's vision.

The first chapter of 1 Enoch uses apocalyptic language drawn from the Old Testament. 1 Enoch 1:4 says, "The Holy Great One will come forth from His dwelling, And the eternal

God will tread upon the earth, (even) on Mount Sinai."
Deuteronomy 33:2 recalls Israel's experience after the Exodus
similarly: "The Lord came from Sinai . . . and he came with ten
thousands of saints." 1 Enoch 1:6 ("And the high mountains shall
be shaken, And the high hills shall be made low, And shall melt
like wax before the flame") evokes imagery from Micah 1:3–4:
"The mountains shall be molten under him, and the valleys
shall be cleft, as wax before the fire." These terrifying events
cause all to tremble, even the angelic watchers.

When the Holy One arrives, he will render judgment on
all people. As 1 Enoch 1:9 states, "He will come with ten millions of his holy ones in order to execute judgment upon all."
Daniel 7:10 describes a dream of the great Day of Judgment in
similar terms, in which "the Ancient of days" has "thousand
thousands ministered unto him, and ten thousand times ten
thousand stood before him." Although Christian readers may
think this Holy One is the coming messiah, in 1 Enoch 1:4–5 the
coming one is identified as the "eternal God" coming from Sinai.

1 Enoch 1:9 sets the theme for the Book of the Watchers:
"Judgment is coming upon all." In the context of Enoch, the
coming judgment is Noah's flood. But the writer is thinking
beyond the Genesis flood to a future judgment of God on the
wicked. Just as God preserved Noah and his family, so, too, will
the righteous elect of the writer's day be preserved from the
coming judgment. Although the wicked will be destroyed, "to
the righteous he will grant peace" (1:8).

1 Enoch 2:1 to 5:4 is wisdom poetry—a kind of ancient Jewish
philosophy that uses various literary devices to express ideas.
The writer invites his readers to think about the orderliness
of creation, and says the natural world proves God is steadfast.
The progression of seasons follows precise patterns and laws. In
5:4 the writer concludes that this orderliness means the wicked
will find no peace: "But as for you, you have not been steadfast,
nor done the commandments of the Lord."

Because they have spoken proud words against the Lord, the wicked will be cursed and perish (5:5). As for the chosen, they will rejoice; they receive forgiveness of sins and peace. "For the elect there shall be light and grace and peace, and they shall inherit the earth." (5:6–7). This phrase is similar to when Jesus says, "The meek shall inherit the earth" (Matthew 5:5). The idea that God's chosen will "inherit the earth" is also found in Isaiah 65:9 and Psalms 37:9.

Enoch says that after the judgment God will give His elect wisdom and they will no longer sin (5:8). This is not immortality, since verse 9 says, "they shall complete the number of the days of their life." This description of long life in the end-times may allude to Isaiah 65:20: "There shall be no more thence an infant of days, nor an old man that hath not filled his days."

Section 2: Chapters 6–11

When I read a novel, sometimes I want to know more than the author tells me. Most people who read *The Lord of the Rings* wonder, "Who is Tom Bombadil?" He is a strange character who implies he is a very powerful, eternal being. As a result, *Lord of the Rings* fans and scholars have long speculated about the origins of the character and who J. R. R. Tolkien thought Tom Bombadil was.

The biblical story of the giants in Genesis 6:1–4 is like this. There is only a tantalizing hint of something mysterious that will ultimately result in God's judgment on the entire world. It says: "And it came to pass, when men began to multiply on the face of the earth, and daughters were born unto them, That the sons of God saw the daughters of men that they were fair; and they took them wives of all which they chose. And the Lord said, 'My spirit shall not always strive with man, for that he also is flesh: yet his days shall be an hundred and twenty years.' There were giants in the earth in those days; and also after

1 ENOCH and JUDE

The New Testament book of Jude used at least two books that were not canonical for either the Jews or Christians. In Jude 14–15, the writer quotes 1 Enoch 1:9 and appears to know the story of the Book of the Watchers. That Jude could *quote* 1 Enoch means the Jewish communities in Judea to whom Jude was writing knew the book. The fragments of 1 Enoch found in the Dead Sea Scrolls, discovered on the northern shore of the Dead Sea, confirm that 1 Enoch was known to the communities there.

The book of Jude addresses a church struggling with people who are ungodly and "pervert the grace of our God into sensuality" (Jude 1:4). Jude compares these ungodly people to "the angels who did not stay within their own position of authority" (Jude 1:6) and are now held in eternal chains until the Day of Judgment. This angelic rebellion is the plot of 1 Enoch 6–19. Some angels lust after human women and produce children, the giants. God therefore destroys creation with a global flood, and the angels are put in chains (1 Enoch 13:1–2) inside the Earth (1 Enoch 14:5).

Christians often explain Jude's use of 1 Enoch the way pastors use popular films or television shows to illustrate points in a sermon. For many, Jude's quotation of 1 Enoch does not imply the book was divinely inspired or worthy of being included in the canon. Rather, they say, Jude used a popular story his readers knew to make a point about the opponents of Christ in his readers' congregations. Since an important theme of the book of Jude is a false teaching that was smuggled into the church, comparing these opponents to the fallen angels in 1 Enoch who are destined for judgment would make a dramatic point.

that, when the sons of God came in unto the daughters of men, and they bare children to them, the same became mighty men which were of old, men of renown" (KJV; the giants are called Nephilim in modern translations). The story shows how far the wickedness of humans has gone: They interacted sexually with spiritual beings. Genesis does not explain how that is possible, but concludes "the wickedness of man was great in the earth, and that every imagination of the thoughts of his heart was only evil continually" (Genesis 6:5).

Who are these giants? Who were the "sons of God" who had children by the daughters of men? Although the Apocrypha mentions the giants several times (Wisdom of Solomon 14:6, Sirach 16:7, and 3 Maccabees 2:4), there are no additional details explaining the story. The second part of the Book of the Watchers offers an explanation.

In 1 Enoch, the "sons of heaven" are angelic beings led by Shemihazah—the name means "my name has seen." "Name" refers to God (in Hebrew he is sometimes known as Hashem—"the name"), suggesting the angel Shemihazah is constantly watching God. Some readers of 1 Enoch think this refers to Satan as the leader of the rebellious angels. As the story progresses, however, another angel, Azazel, emerges as the ringleader of the rebels. Later in the book, Enoch will intercede on behalf of Azazel. When reading 1 Enoch, it is important to avoid imposing later Christian theology onto 1 Enoch. Azazel is not Enoch's version of Satan.

This expansion of the biblical story of the giants blames wicked angelic beings for revealing mysteries to humans that will cause sin. It is not Adam's rebellion in Eden that introduces evil into creation, but these wicked angelic beings who do not stick to their appointed role. The great flood is not the result of human sin, either, but the rebellion of these angelic beings.

KEY VERSES

"And all the others together with them took unto themselves wives, and each chose for himself one, and they began to go in unto them and to defile themselves with them, and they taught them charms and enchantments, and the cutting of roots, and made them acquainted with plants. And they became pregnant, and they bare great giants, whose height was [three hundred cubits]: Who consumed all the acquisitions of men. And when men could no longer sustain them, the giants turned against them and devoured mankind."

1 ENOCH 7:1–4

COMMENTARY

In the days of Enoch's father, Jared, two hundred rebellious angels take an oath to descend to Mount Hermon to find women to marry and have children with. Mount Hermon is the tallest mountain on the northern border of Canaan. In Canaanite mythology, it was the home of the gods. 1 Enoch 6:7–8 lists the names of the twenty leaders of the rebellious angels. Most have names that refer to God (for example, Remashel, "evening of God," and Kokabel, "star of God").

In chapters 7 and 8, the angels make good on their plan and take women as wives. The children of the angels are giants, three hundred cubits (450 feet!) tall. These giants eat so much food that the humans can no longer provide enough for them. Therefore, the giants eat humans and all other kinds of animals. 1 Enoch 7:3 says the giants drank the blood of animals—a serious departure from law, as laid out in Deuteronomy 12:23.

The rebellious angels teach humans various practices that may lead to sin, such as medicinal magic and how to interpret a wide range of celestial signs. The angel Azazel teaches humans the art of metalworking, including making weapons. Azazel also teaches humans to make eye shadow and other physical ornamentation. Other angels teach the humans how to track the stars (astrology and divination). Humanity cries out because the giants are killing them, and their cry "goes up to heaven."

In 1 Enoch 9 we learn that four angels, Michael, Sariel, Raphael, and Gabriel, are watching the progress of the events on Earth. In the New Testament, Michael is an archangel (a chief angel) and Gabriel announces Jesus's birth to the Virgin Mary. Raphael appears in the apocryphal book Tobit. Although they are not called archangels in 1 Enoch, later Catholic tradition considers Michael, Raphael, and Gabriel to be archangels. Later Jewish tradition lists Uriel as the fourth; in 1 Enoch 40:9 Phanuel is the fourth.

These four angels hear the cries of the humans and respond in prayer. They tell God Azazel has revealed the eternal mysteries that are in heaven (9:6). They blame Shemihazah for allowing the other angels to have sex with the humans and produce the hybrid giants.

God responds to this prayer in chapter 10 by sending out the angels with specific tasks. Sariel is sent to Noah to warn him of the coming flood and to instruct Noah on how to flee from the Flood and "preserve his seed for all generations." Gabriel is sent to destroy the children of the angels. These giants are described as "bastards and children of adultery" who had hoped to live for five hundred years (1 Enoch 10:10).

Raphael is sent to bind Azazel's hands and feet and to throw him into the darkness. (Both Jude 6 and 2 Peter 2:4–5 refer to angels who fell as "bound in chains in darkness.") Michael is sent to warn Shemihazah that he is about to be judged and be bound for eighty generations under the mountains, in a pit of fire, until the Day of Judgment. In Revelation 20:1–3 an angel binds Satan with a great chain and locks him in a bottomless pit.

After the coming judgment, God will cleanse the world of all pollution and the righteous will flourish (10:22). There will be great agricultural blessings, and "every vine will yield a thousand jugs of wine" (10:19). God will open his "storehouse of blessing" to inaugurate a time when "peace and truth shall become partners again in all the days of the world and in all the generations of the earth" (11:1–2).

Section 3: Chapters 12–16

After telling the story of the rebellious angels and the origin of the giants, 1 Enoch 12 introduces the reader to Enoch for the first time. The author presents Enoch as a true prophet of God, in the tradition of Isaiah and Ezekiel. Enoch is a "righteous man and scribe of truth" (15:1) who ascends to the throne room of God. Like an Old Testament prophet, he is given a specific task: to pronounce judgment on the watchers who have oppressed humans and introduced sinful practices. At the end of this section, Enoch begins his cosmic journey through the heavens.

There are a few developments in this section to look for as you read. First, Enoch is a prophet and intercessor between the rebellious watchers and God. The introduction to the book presented Enoch as being like Moses. Like Moses at Mount Sinai receiving the law directly from God, Enoch receives God's word directly. When the people of Israel sinned in the wilderness, God punished them. Moses interceded before God on behalf of the people and God relented. Like Moses, Enoch asks forgiveness for the rebellious watchers.

Second, God's judgment is inescapable. Unlike the people of Israel in the wilderness, God will not forgive the rebellious watchers. They will never again ascend to heaven and are destined to be bound in the Earth for all eternity (14:5).

WHO ARE the WATCHERS?

Since 1 Enoch calls the rebellious angels "watchers" several times, chapters 1 to 36 are usually titled the Book of the Watchers. But the term "watcher" is applied to holy angels as well. In 22:6, Raphael is called a "watcher and holy one." Although some of the watchers are rebellious angels, 1 Enoch never describes them as demons.

Since the Aramaic word translated as "watcher" in Daniel can also mean "awake," these angels are always awake and watching God's activities. Similar divine beings appear in Canaanite and Babylonian mythology. Because they are always watching and serving God, the medieval Jewish scholar Rashi suggested they do not have knees, since they do not need to sit.

Watchers appear in other apocalyptic literature. In Daniel 4, an angelic being is called "watcher" several times. Although they are not called watchers, the Old Testament prophet Ezekiel describes the cherubim as "full of eyes all round about them," suggesting these angelic beings are always watching (Ezekiel 1:18). Watchers appear in other early Jewish literature, such as the Book of Jubilees and parts of the Dead Sea Scrolls. Because of their similarities to cherubim, some scholars suggest the four living creatures in Revelation 4:6 are watchers.

Some scholars have suggested the Book of the Watchers reflects the struggles of the Jewish people against the Greek rulers in Israel, who devoured local resources and introduced what the writer considers sinful practices. The illicit marriages of the watchers may be a criticism of the lack of purity of priests before the Maccabean Revolt. Clearly, Enoch sees evil in his day as being the result of dark spiritual forces.

Third, this section contributes to the author's view of the origins of evil. When the giants are destroyed, they become the evil spirits who violently oppress humans (15:8–11). Although evil spirits are rare in the Old Testament, by the first century BCE Judaism had developed a complicated demonology. The Testament of Solomon (a pseudepigraphical text) from the first century BCE is a catalog of demons with suggested methods to cast them out. The Book of the Watchers contributes to this developing theology of evil beings.

Fourth, the rebellious watchers have forsaken their place in God's heavenly sanctuary to defile themselves with women (15:3–4). As I suggested in the previous section, 1 Enoch may be telling the story of the watchers to critique the priesthood in the writer's own day. In a commentary on 1 Enoch, one scholar points out parallels to Ezra, a scribe who also interceded on behalf of Jerusalem and criticized the priests of his day for marrying foreign women. The biblical book of Ezra predates 1 Enoch, and there are other similar criticisms of the Temple priests in the first and second centuries BCE.

KEY VERSE

"From the days of the slaughter and destruction and death of the giants, from the souls of whose flesh the spirits, having gone forth, shall destroy without incurring judgment—thus shall they destroy until the day of the consummation, the great judgment in which the age shall be consummated, over the watchers and the godless, yea, shall be wholly consummated."

1 ENOCH 16:1

COMMENTARY

This section begins with Enoch praying before the Lord of majesty. God tells him to go to the rebellious watchers and deliver a message: Because they have forsaken their place in heaven and defiled themselves with human women, they will have no peace or forgiveness (1 Enoch 12).

Enoch delivers this message to Azazel, the leader of the rebellious watchers. All the watchers are terrified, and they ask Enoch to plead their case before God, so Enoch writes out a petition asking for forgiveness and longevity for the watchers. He reads this petition in the presence of the Lord, but, unlike Moses's successful intercession in the Old Testament, God does not relent from his punishment of the watchers.

So far, we do not know the content of God's message that Enoch brought to the rebellious watchers. Beginning in chapter 14, though, Enoch reveals the vision he received concerning God's judgment of the watchers. The rebellious watchers will be bound in a place where they will "groan and beg forever over the destruction of their children, and there shall not be peace for them even forever" (14:5–6). This punishment is described in more detail later in the book.

1 Enoch 14:7–16:4 describes Enoch's ascent to heaven, where he learns about the punishment of the watchers. He is caught up in clouds and fog, where he sees a great house surrounded by tongues of fire, shooting stars, and lightning. The great house is built of white marble and lined with mosaics, with a crystal-like floor. There are fiery cherubim guarding the burning gates. Enoch is terrified by this vision and trembles greatly as he falls on his face.

A door opens and he sees a lofty throne with the Great Glory sitting upon it. The throne itself is encircled by flames. The Great Glory is dressed like a man, but he has the appearance of the sun. The one seated on the throne is so great that not even the angels can look upon him. Ten thousand times ten thousand beings stand before him as servants.

The author of 1 Enoch draws on several throne visions in the Old Testament for this section. Both Isaiah 6 and Ezekiel 1–3 describe a great throne in heaven. The thrones are also surrounded by fire and smoke and the one seated on the throne is indescribable. Both visions include angelic creatures, the seraphim and cherubim, who guard the throne of God. Revelation 4–5 may have been influenced by Enoch's vision of God's throne. Just as in Isaiah and Ezekiel, Enoch is unable to stand when he sees this vision of the throne. He lies facedown before the throne until the Lord calls him and lifts Enoch up to speak with him.

1 Enoch 15–16 reports God's judgment on the rebellious watchers. They are condemned because they abandoned their place in the heavenly sanctuary, took human wives, and had children with them. It is important to understand the nature of this rebellion. Enoch does not say women are evil or that human sexuality is sinful. In 1 Enoch 15:5 God says he gave women to men so that they can have children and fill the Earth (Genesis 1:28). The watchers' rebellion is abandoning the heavenly role God assigned to them.

Their children, the giants, become evil spirits on the Earth (15:8–12). These spirits will continue to be corrupt until the great age when everything is concluded (16:1). Although this refers to the great flood of Noah, the author of 1 Enoch antici-pates a Day of Judgment in his own future when wickedness will finally be destroyed.

DEMONS in EARLY JUDAISM

Demons have been popular subjects in Hollywood. *The Exorcist* (1973) terrified audiences with graphic scenes of demonic possession. *The Exorcism of Emily Rose* (2005) compared demon possession and mental illness. People are fascinated by demons and the origin of evil in this world, even if these movies are more shocking than theologically accurate.

According to 1 Enoch 15, when the bodies of the giants were destroyed in the Flood, evil spirits were released into the world. These evil spirits roam the Earth and commit violence against humans. The Old Testament says remarkably little about demons and nothing about their origin, although both Deuteronomy 32:17 and Psalms 106:37 refer to demons and false gods. Leviticus 17:7, which speaks of goat gods or satyrs, may refer to Azazel, the leader of the rebellious watchers—although many scholars suggest Azazel is a place-name rather than a demon.

Starting with 1 Enoch in the third century BCE, early Judaism began to develop the idea of demons into a complex theology of evil. In the apocryphal book of Tobit, Tobias casts a demon from his future wife by burning a fish liver (Tobit 8:2–3). The Testament of Solomon is a catalog of demons, listing each demon's name, the illness associated with the demon, and methods for casting the demon out of the afflicted person. The Jewish historian Josephus (37–101 CE) tells the story of Eleazer, a Jewish exorcist who used a magic ring to cast out demons. Acts 19:11–20 describes the activity of Jewish exorcists in Ephesus who try (and fail) to cast out demons in the name of Jesus.

Section 4: Chapters 17–19

I have always been fascinated with maps, especially old maps depicting unknown lands. Ancient maps were more ideological than practical. The oldest known map of the world is a Babylonian map from the sixth century BCE showing the great cities of Mesopotamia surrounded by a chaotic ocean. The message was clear: Babylon was at the center of the world. Old maps sometimes put the words "here be dragons" in unexplored territory or added mermaids and sea monsters to unknown oceans. The Bunting Clover Leaf Map, published in 1581, shows Jerusalem at the center of three continents surrounded by ocean, complete with a mermaid and the god Triton.

In 1 Enoch 17, Enoch begins his tour of the cosmos, heaven, and the place of judgment. Like the Babylonian world map, the geography in this section is not literal. The author of 1 Enoch is expressing an ancient understanding of the orderliness of the universe. In the Old Testament book of Job, the author describes heavenly storehouses for snow and hail and the foundation of the Earth. Like Job, Enoch's geography expresses a theological viewpoint: God is in control of the entire cosmos.

As you read these chapters, here are some themes to look for. First, apocalyptic literature often describes a "heavenly tour." Like the great prophets Isaiah and Ezekiel, Enoch is given a tour of the universe, from the central heavenly mountain to the very edges of the world, where he will see the terrifying place of the rebellious watchers' torment.

Second, books like 1 Enoch use angels to guide the prophet and answer his questions. After Enoch sees seven stars burning like mountains, the angel Uriel explains that the stars are the spirits of the angels who defiled themselves. Sometimes Enoch will ask questions about what he is seeing, and Uriel will explain what the vision is.

Third, the major theme of Enoch's heavenly tour is the fulfillment of the judgment on the rebellious watchers. In the previous section, Enoch delivered a message of God's judgment. Beginning in this section, Enoch sees the place where God imprisoned the rebellious angels and he witnesses their punishment.

Fourth, even though the watchers are punished, God's judgment on the rebellious angels does not end evil in the world. In the original biblical story of the Flood, the destruction of the giants does not end human rebellion against God. Rather than fill the Earth after the Flood, as commanded, humans congregate on the plain of Shinar and build the Tower of Babel (Genesis 11). Keep in mind 1 Enoch is concerned with Jewish people living in the second century BCE. The writer thinks people in his day are just as rebellious.

KEY VERSES

"And they took and brought me to a place in which those who were there were like flaming fire, and when they wished, they appeared as men. And they brought me to the place of darkness, and to a mountain the point of whose summit reached to heaven. And I saw the places of the luminaries and the treasuries of the stars and of the thunder, and in the uttermost depths, where were a fiery bow and arrows and their quiver, and a fiery sword and all the lightning."

1 ENOCH 17:1–3

COMMENTARY

1 Enoch 17–19 recounts Enoch's journey through the heavens. In his first vision, there are several scenes reflecting an ancient worldview that graphically depicts how God maintains the

orderly universe. These chapters may also reflect an aspect of ancient Near Eastern diplomacy: A king often showed his wealth and strength to impress visiting diplomats. In the Old Testament, Solomon showed off his wealth to the Queen of Sheba. Hezekiah showed ambassadors from Babylon all the treasures in his storehouses. Enoch is shown God's wealth and power, making the rebellion of the watchers appear even more foolish.

His journey begins when he is led to a place where he meets beings like flaming fire who can appear as humans whenever they like. These are angelic beings, possibly the seraphim mentioned in Isaiah 6:2, since the Hebrew word can refer to glowing or burning. Enoch is shown the treasuries of the stars where thunder and lightning are stored, and he sees the fires of the west where sunsets are stored. He sees a river of fire that flows into the great sea. Some scholars associate this with the Greek underworld, which was bounded by the rivers Phlegethon, Styx, Lethe, and Cocytus. Plato said the Phlegethon flowed into Tartarus, the deep abyss used as a prison for the Titans.

In chapter 17, Enoch sees the storehouse of the wind, the cornerstone of the Earth, and the pillars of heaven. Many ancient Near Eastern cultures thought of the universe as a building or a temple. This is also true for ancient Judaism. The pillars of the Earth are mentioned often in the Old Testament, as is the cornerstone of the Earth. Some biblical scholars think Genesis describes the Garden of Eden as a temple. Enoch, too, sees all of creation as God's temple.

As his journey continues, Enoch sees seven mountains made of various precious stones—three to the east and three to the south, all ringed with fire. The central peak is the throne of God. It is made of antimony (a silvery metal) and is topped with a throne made of lapis lazuli (a deep blue semiprecious stone), although some translations render this as sapphire (which is usually blue). This fiery mountaintop throne evokes God's presence; in Exodus 24:10, the ground at Mount Sinai is sapphire, and in Ezekiel 1:26 God's throne appears to be sapphire.

Having gone beyond the mountains to the edge of the Earth, Enoch sees an immeasurable pit with heavenly fire (18:12-15; 19:1-2). Uriel, the angel accompanying Enoch, explains the pit is the place where the stars and powers of heaven are imprisoned because they did not keep to their appointed roles. They will remain in prison for ten thousand years, until their sins are fully punished.

What about the humans who married the rebellious watchers? Uriel explains that the spirits of the dead giants (their offspring) assume many forms and will lead humans to sacrifice to demons. There are a few passages in the Old Testament that relate idolatry to the worship of demons (Psalms 106:37). This view appears in the New Testament as well (1 Corinthians 10:20). 1 Enoch 19:2 says that the wives of the rebellious watchers will become sirens. In Greek mythology, sirens are half birds and half women who seduce sailors and cause shipwrecks.

Section 5: Chapters 20–27

Contemporary culture is fascinated by angels. The Christmas favorite *It's a Wonderful Life* follows a guardian angel hoping to earn his wings. The popular television show *Touched by an Angel* ran for nine seasons; in each episode an angel helped some human with their problems. More recently, the miniseries *Good Omens* tells the story of an angel and a demon who join forces to stop the apocalypse. These types of popular entertainment present angels as active in this world, protecting humans and helping them live better lives.

These stories are far from the biblical view of angels. Most of the Old Testament does not say much about angels or their activities—the Old Testament gives the names of only two (Gabriel and Michael, both in the book of Daniel).

HADES, the ABYSS, and TARTARUS

In popular culture, people imagine that when wicked people die, they are sent to hell, where they experience ironic tortures related to the sins they committed during their life. One of my favorite *Far Side* cartoons shows a demon leading a great classical music conductor into a room full of banjo players. "Welcome to Hell, maestro," says the demon. These humorous depictions of hell are more indebted to Dante's *Inferno* than either Jewish or Christian scripture, and the medieval theology in Dante may reflect the books of Enoch.

In this section, Enoch describes the world as surrounded by water gushing forth from "the mouth of the deep." In Genesis 1 the world is formless and void, engulfed in chaotic waters. When the Hebrew Bible was translated into Greek, the translators used the word "abyss" for this chaotic ocean. The word itself has the sense of an incredible deep hole. The common word for the place of the dead in the Old Testament is *"sheol,"* a gloomy land. For this reason, some early Jewish literature used "abyss" as the counterpart to "heaven" (Psalms 107:26).

As we saw in this section, Enoch uses this language for the prison of the rebellious angels. They are held in a dark place beyond the edge of the world. The New Testament uses similar words for the place where demons are held prisoner. 2 Peter 2:4 may allude to the story of 1 Enoch. The writer says God cast the angels who sinned into "hell," but the Greek word is "Tartarus." The Greeks thought Tartarus was a bottomless pit lower than Hades. In Revelation 9, the abyss is the source of demonic, locust-like creatures. Later in Revelation, the beast rises from the sea (11:7; 17:8) and the abyss will be the place of Satan's imprisonment during the messiah's reign on Earth (20:1–3).

Jewish thinking about angels became more complex during the time between the Old and New Testaments, and 1 Enoch reflects an early stage in the development of the theology of angels. As you have seen, the writer of Enoch interpreted the "sons of God" in Genesis 6:2 as angelic beings. This section of Enoch lists seven archangels and their specific duties. Enoch also describes several other kinds of angels: the seraphim, cherubim, and ophanim. Some of these angels relate to the function of the sun, moon, and stars. 2 Enoch describes even more classes and ranks of angels. 3 Enoch has a list of archangels with different names and roles and introduces Metatron, the mightiest of all the angels.

There are several important themes to keep in mind as you read 1 Enoch 20–27. First, notice that some archangels listed in chapter 20 accompany Enoch on his journey and answer his questions. Uriel, Michael, and Gabriel appear often in 1 Enoch; others are not mentioned again.

Second, this section of 1 Enoch expands the description of the place of torment. For the first time in the book, the spirits of sinners are buried in the Earth and tortured until the great Day of Judgment.

Third, this section of 1 Enoch alludes to several themes from the Old Testament. Enoch sees the spirit of Abel (who was murdered by his brother, Cain). When he visits the throne of God, Enoch also sees a wonderful fragrant tree, likely the Tree of Life from Genesis.

Finally, these chapters offer evidence for an early Jewish belief (by the first century CE) in the idea of resurrection. We know not all Jews believed in resurrection of the dead or a great Day of Judgment. But 1 Enoch demonstrates some Jewish thinkers did believe in both resurrection and a final judgment.

KEY VERSES

"And I proceeded to where things were chaotic. And I saw there something horrible: I saw neither a heaven above nor a firmly founded earth, but a place chaotic and horrible. And there I saw seven stars of the heaven bound together in it, like great mountains and burning with fire."

1 ENOCH 21:1–3

COMMENTARY

Chapter 20 is a list of the names of the archangels and their functions:

- Uriel ("light of God"), who oversees the world and Tartarus, the prison where the rebellious watchers are kept

- Raphael ("God heals"), who oversees the spirits of humans

- Reuel ("shepherd of God"), who takes vengeance on the world for the luminaries—the rebellious watchers

- Michael ("who is like God?"), who is benevolent toward the Jewish people

- Sariel ("God's prince"), who is set over the spirits of humans who sin in the spirit

- Gabriel ("man of God"), who oversees paradise, the serpents, and the cherubim

- Remiel ("thunder of God"), who guides souls to heaven

What is the point of listing the names and functions of these angels? Unlike the rebellious watchers, these angels did not abandon the place God assigned them. In 21:5 Uriel is called the leader of the archangels, although in other Jewish literature

Michael is the leader who will rise in the last days to defend the Jewish people (Daniel 12). In the New Testament, only Michael is called an archangel (Jude 9) and he fights a war in heaven against Satan (Revelation 12:7).

After the list of the seven archangels, Enoch travels to the terrible prison of the seven fallen angels. The place is a narrow cleft filled with a great fire. Enoch cannot estimate the size of the place, but he is terrified by the sight. Uriel tells him the fallen angels will be confined forever.

The rest of this section is Enoch's second journey. In this vision, Enoch travels to the place of punishment of the fallen stars, which are the fallen angels. He sees a chaotic and terrible place in which seven stars as large as mountains are bound. When Enoch asks who the stars are, Uriel chastises him for his eagerness. The angel explains the place is a prison-house for the angels who rebelled.

On the west side of a great mountain, Enoch sees a place where the dead assemble until the Day of Judgment (chapter 22). Enoch sees the spirit of Abel crying out for the God to wipe Cain's descendants from the Earth.

From there Enoch continues to the west, where he sees the tracks of the sun, the "fire burning in the west" (chapter 23). He sees seven other mountains made of precious stones, each more glorious than the next. The greatest of these summits is the throne on which God will sit when he visits the Earth with goodness (25:3).

On this greatest mountain is a fragrant tree that no human can touch until after the judgment. This is probably the Tree of Life from the Garden of Eden. Enoch says the fragrance of this tree is sweeter than all spices, and its leaves and blossoms are lovely. The righteous will be permitted to eat the fruit of the tree, and the fragrance of the tree will penetrate their bones so that they live a long life on the Earth, "as your fathers lived in their days."

This is a significant passage in the first section of Enoch because it looks forward to a time when God will visit the Earth and begin a period of peace. This future, peaceful kingdom theme becomes more important later in Enoch.

Finally, the angels take Enoch to the center of the Earth, the city of Jerusalem (chapter 26). Remember, this is a theological geography that puts Jerusalem at the center of the map. A stream of water flows out of the holy mountain in several directions, like the description of the Temple in Ezekiel 47 and Revelation 22:1–5. From this vantage point, Enoch can see a desolate land with deep valleys and no trees growing in them. Enoch asks Uriel about this desolate land and the angel explains this is where those who cursed the Lord are kept.

Section 6: Chapters 28–32

How do people show off their wealth? In Western culture, wealthy people may have several large houses in exclusive neighborhoods, expensive cars, and yachts. The wealthy eat in elegant restaurants and wear only designer clothes. The popular television show *Lifestyles of the Rich and Famous* used the phrase "champagne wishes and caviar dreams" to describe their lavish lives.

At this point in 1 Enoch, the prophet is traveling to the East to see the paradise of the righteous, the Garden of Eden God made for the first humans, Adam and Eve. By the time 1 Enoch was written, the gardens of the great kings of the East were called paradise—pleasure gardens where they showed off their wealth. Imagine a Palace of Versailles on steroids. The garden of a great king encompassed manicured lawns and beautiful trees and plants from all over the world to show off his immense wealth.

The writer of 1 Enoch wants to describe the Garden of Eden as the most impressive paradise anyone could imagine. As Enoch approaches the garden, he encounters a series of

THE TREE of LIFE

According to Genesis, there were two special trees in the Garden of Eden: the Tree of Life and the Tree of the Knowledge of Good and Evil. When Adam and Eve rebelled and ate from the Tree of Knowledge of Good and Evil, God exiled them from Eden, and they no longer had access to the Tree of Life. Other than Genesis, the only references in the Old Testament to a Tree of Life are in Proverbs 3:18 in which wisdom is "a tree of life to those who grasp her." Some Mesopotamian myths describe magical trees in a divine garden, but there is no consensus among scholars on how to interpret this symbolism or its relationship (if any) to Genesis.

Like 1 Enoch, some early Jewish writings compare a future time of peace and prosperity to the Garden of Eden. According to the pseudepigraphic Testament of Levi from the second century BCE, a time is coming when God will open the gates of paradise and allow the righteous to eat from the Tree of Life. The Jewish apocalypse book 4 Ezra from the late first century looks forward to the new age when paradise is opened and the Tree of Life is planted. This will seal up evil and banish illness and death.

The New Testament mentions the Tree of Life only in Revelation. As in 1 Enoch and the other early Jewish texts, the Tree of Life is part of a heavenly New Jerusalem, where God will give the righteous the right to eat from it (Revelation 22:14).

mountains covered in fragrant trees bearing spices. Although most modern readers find this strange, spices were the "champagne wishes and caviar dreams" of the ancient world. Only the wealthy could afford to use spices imported from distant lands for their incense and perfumes. But even the wealthiest person in the ancient world did not have cinnamon trees growing in their garden, let along an entire mountain covered with them. This section of Enoch is showing off the incredible wealth and power of God in a way that would impress the ancient world.

As you travel with Enoch on this brief tour of the fragrant trees and the paradise of God, here are some things to look for. First, try to imagine how the first readers of 1 Enoch might hear the descriptions of mountains of spice trees surrounding God's paradise of righteousness.

Second, this section of 1 Enoch describes paradise, or the Garden of Eden. It is likely you will have more questions than answers after reading the brief descriptions of the spice trees as Enoch approaches the Paradise of the Righteous. Does the paradise described in this section refer to the place where God lives? Or does he only occasionally visit the garden, as in the biblical story?

KEY VERSE

"And I came to the Garden of Righteousness, and saw beyond those trees many large trees growing there and of goodly fragrance, large, very beautiful and glorious, and the tree of wisdom whereof they eat and know great wisdom."

1 ENOCH 32:3

COMMENTARY

As Enoch approaches paradise, he encounters fragrant trees bearing various spices (1 Enoch 28:1–3). Some of these varieties are well known, but others are difficult to translate, or the textual evidence is unclear. You may see some different words in this section depending on which translation of 1 Enoch you are reading.

Why does Enoch include this list of eleven spices? There are several possibilities. A common suggestion is the list is based on the list of ingredients for incense and anointing oil in Exodus 30:22–38. Similar spices appear in the Talmud.

Another possibility is to remind the reader of worship in the Temple. Some of these spices were burned as incense during worship. When Solomon built the Temple, it was decorated with cherubim, trees, and flowers. As Enoch approaches the Paradise of the Righteous, the writer describes the heavenly Temple in the Garden of Eden.

A third possibility is to highlight the wealth of the garden of God. Spices were expensive commodities in the ancient world. Only the wealthy could afford the spices growing on these mountains. Many of them were used as perfumes. In Song of Solomon 3:6, the beloved bride is like a locked garden growing many choice spices, including nard, cinnamon, myrrh, and frankincense. Proverbs 7:17 lists some of these spices as perfumes used for seduction.

The Bible mentions frankincense and myrrh frequently. Both were gifts of the Magi. Mastic is a resin from the island of Chios, although the Greek version of 1 Enoch uses a word better translated as calamus, a spice reed used in perfumes and medicines. Cinnamon is the best known of these spices to modern readers, although in the ancient world cinnamon was used for incense and perfume.

Sarara is often translated as balm. The word refers to a fragrant resin with a pleasant lilac scent, probably storax balsam.

Galbanum is only mentioned in the list of incense ingredients in Exodus 30:24 and had a sharp smell.

Contemporary use of aloe vera differs slightly from the use of the bark of aloe trees in the ancient world. Although used for perfume and medicinal purposes, when mixed with myrrh, aloe was used for burial (John 19:39) and embalming.

The next tree is "full of stacte" in older editions of 1 Enoch, but "bark of almond trees" in more recent translations. The Greek word "stacte" refers to dripping oil, so this may be oil from myrrh or oil from bitter almonds.

"Excellent nard" is a perfume used by both men and women; it's made from the spikenard plant from the Himalayas. This may account for the slight detour to the northwest in 1 Enoch 32:1. In Mark 14, a woman uses perfume made from nard worth nearly a year's wages to anoint Jesus's feet.

Since cinnamon trees appeared earlier in the list, most modern translations of 1 Enoch translate the next spice as cardamom. Cardamom is made from seeds of a plant native to India, so it fits well with the rest of the spices on the list. But if this is cardamom, it is the only spice that does not appear in the Old Testament.

Finally, pepper was native to India. Pepper was a condiment in the ancient world, but was also used for medicinal purposes.

1 Enoch 32:2 is another case where translations differ. Older translations say Enoch approached the Erythraean Sea. This is the Greek name for the Red Sea. The name can refer to the modern Persian Gulf, Red Sea, or even the Indian Ocean. Older translations say Enoch passed over "the angel Zotiel," but more recent scholars translate this as "crossed over the darkness." If this refers to an angel, its name would mean "the blaze of God," leading some to suggest this is the angel who barred the way back to Eden in Genesis 3:24. However, it is more likely

Ethiopic manuscripts have corrupted the Greek word for "gloomy darkness," which is a common adjective in 1 Enoch.

In 33:3–4, Enoch finally arrives at the Paradise of the Righteous. Since paradise refers to a garden, Enoch sees even more large and beautiful trees, including the Tree of Wisdom. In the biblical story of Eden, there is a Tree of the Knowledge of Good and Evil, rather than a Tree of Wisdom. Like Eve, Enoch observes that the tree is beautiful. Gabriel reminds Enoch that this is the tree Adam and Eve ate from and learned wisdom and, as a result, were driven from the garden.

Section 7: Chapters 33–36

This section of 1 Enoch reminds me of a famous story told by people as diverse as philosopher David Hume, astrophysicist Stephen Hawking, and novelist Terry Pratchett. A child asks his father, "On what does the world stand?" The father tells his child the world stands on the back of a turtle. Not satisfied with the answer, the child asks what that turtle stands on, and the father says the turtle stands on the back of another turtle. The child presses on: What does that turtle stand on? Exasperated, the father finally says, "It's turtles all the way down!"

Like the child in that story, ancient people wondered what the world stood on, what held up the sky, and what was beyond the edge of the world. In Egyptian mythology, the edge of the world was the entrance to the Netherworld. In Mesopotamian myth, the western edge of the world was the place of immortality and wisdom, but to the east was the underworld. Both the east and the west had gates guarded by gods. Anyone trying to reach these gates encountered strange animals and plants on the way.

Enoch completes his journey through the heavens and arrives at the ends of the Earth. Like the rest of the Book of the Watchers, this section reflects an ancient view of the world.

PARADISE and HEAVEN

In Genesis 2:8-9, God planted the original Garden of Eden and filled it with all kinds of beautiful fruit trees. The garden was watered by four rivers. Later Jewish readers lived in the dry Middle East, so they would think of Eden as a place of abundance beyond their imagination. The Garden of Eden was the place where God made humans and walked with them in the cool of the evening. Eden is therefore an ideal physical and spiritual environment.

In the biblical story, Eden is called a garden. This word was commonly used for an oasis, a vegetable garden, or a place with agriculture. Eden was not called paradise until after the Old Testament. 1 Enoch 32 may be the earliest use of the word "paradise" to mean the Garden of Eden. The Hebrew language borrowed the word from Persian. The Persian word originally referred to an enclosed area like a park, a garden, or even an orchard. When the Hebrew Bible was translated into Greek in the second century BCE, the translators chose the Greek word "paradise" for the Garden of Eden in Genesis.

Since apocalyptic literature often describes paradise as hidden in the heavens until the end of the age, the earthly Garden of Eden becomes the heavenly home of the righteous. In 1 Enoch, the righteous will live in paradise, where they will eat from the Tree of Life and the Tree of Wisdom. 2 Enoch 8 calls paradise an "indescribably pleasant" place filled with trees yielding every kind of food, tended by three hundred angels. Like the Enoch literature, Revelation 2:7 says the one who overcomes will enter paradise and eat from the Tree of Life. Jesus reflects this Jewish view of paradise in Luke 23:43 when he tells the thief beside him on the cross, "Today you will be with me in paradise."

The Earth is like a disk covered by the canopy of the skies. In the King James version of Genesis 1:6, this canopy is the firmament—the expanse, in modern translations. Enoch sees great beasts and mythic birds at the edge of the world.

Here are a few things to look for as you read this final section of the Book of the Watchers. First, these chapters suggest Enoch has hidden knowledge. In fact, this knowledge is revealed in the Book of Astronomical Writings (chapters 72–82). If you are interested, skip ahead to that section of this commentary.

Second, this section is a brief ancient astronomical text. The stars can be numbered and named and their movements tracked to determine months. As we will see later, 1 Enoch is interested in the calendar to determine the correct dates for Jewish holy days. Third, as Enoch travels, he sees the gates of heaven, from which various types of weather emerge. This section is like the Lord's speech in Job 38. Job does not describe any gates, but like 1 Enoch, there are storehouses of snow, hail, and lightning. You may want to review Job 38 as you read 1 Enoch 34–36.

KEY VERSES

"And from thence I went towards the north to the ends of the earth, and there I saw a great and glorious device at the ends of the whole earth. And here I saw three portals of heaven open in the heavens: through each of them proceed north winds: when they blow there is cold, hail, frost, snow, dew, and rain."

1 ENOCH 34:1–2

COMMENTARY

At the ends of the Earth, Enoch sees the magnificent beasts and birds. Although these beasts and birds are simply mentioned, there are several ways to understand the reference. First, it is possible the great beasts and beautiful birds are what one would expect to see in a great king's garden. King Solomon's wealth included peacocks and apes (1 Kings 10:22). Paintings in the famous Tomb of Rekhmire (an eighteenth-dynasty Egyptian nobleman, 1479–1425 BCE) depict Nubians bringing giraffes and monkeys to Egypt. The Babylonian king Nebuchadnezzar collected animals from all over his empire.

Second, these great beasts and beautiful birds may reflect ancient Mesopotamian mythology. For example, Gilgamesh encountered scorpion people as he traveled to meet Utnapishtim, the only survivor of the great flood. Enoch does not say enough about these animals to determine whether they are mythical beasts.

Third, it is possible the great beasts and beautiful birds are like ancient histories and travel reports. Travelers returning from distant lands often describe "a variety of beasts and monsters." The Greek historian Herodotus (550–479 BCE) reported the existence of griffins. In the first century CE Pliny the Elder wrote that "griffins were said to lay eggs in burrows on the ground and these nests contained gold nuggets." Herodotus and Pliny both reported on a sacred bird in Egypt, the phoenix.

Moving to the east, Enoch sees the gates of heaven opened and the stars of heaven coming out. Enoch records the names, ranks, seats, periods, and months of their coming and going. The angel Uriel explains all this to him, although at this point in 1 Enoch we do not know what Enoch wrote. Since the Book of Astronomical Writings reveals these secrets, many scholars now suggest that book originally followed the Book of the Watchers.

The Book of the Watchers ends with worship. 1 Enoch 36:4 is a doxology summarizing the great and glorious things God revealed to him. The physical effects of creation are miracles that manifest the power of angels. God's power in creation should lead people to praise God and respect his great works. Because he has seen the Lord of Glory, Enoch says he will continue to bless him forever.

Many scholars think 1 Enoch 81–82, the final chapters of the Book of Astronomical Writings, originally followed the Book of the Watchers. In those chapters, God allows Enoch to see the heavenly tablets containing the sins of humanity. If these two chapters were originally part of the Book of Astronomical Writings, we would expect the tablets to contain astronomical information. A heavenly record of sin fits better after the Book of the Watchers, since a key theme of the section is coming judgment on the rebellious watchers. In this commentary I will discuss chapters 81–82 in the context of the Book of Astronomical Writings.

ANCIENT WORLDVIEWS

In Genesis 1:6-8, God creates an expanse that separates the waters in the sky and the waters on Earth. The word translated as "expanse" is the dome of the sky, as if the sky was an enormous, inverted bowl over the flat Earth. In the biblical story, God creates the sun, moon, and stars and places them in the expanse, and the birds also fly in the expanse (Genesis 1:14-20).

People in the ancient Near East thought they lived on a single continent shaped like a flat disk encircled by the sea. Under the Earth was the Netherworld where the dead live. Above, the sky was a solid dome, like a roof or canopy for the Earth. In Egypt, the vault of heaven is the body of the goddess Nut stretched out over the Earth with her body covered in stars. The Mesopotamian creation myth, Enuma Elish, claims the mountains hold up the sky (which was made from half of the chaos monster Tiamat's corpse). Like Genesis 1, there is no distinction between the sky in which the birds fly and where the stars are.

1 Enoch has a similar view of the world. Both the Netherworld and the Paradise of the Righteous are beyond the edge of the world. The stars enter the sky in the east and exit in the west. Stars govern weather and are used to calculate months and years.

But as we have seen in previous sections, Enoch is describing a theological view of the universe, not a literal description of reality. Enoch places Jerusalem in the center of a flat world disk to emphasize the importance of Jerusalem in creation, not because the world is literally flat.

BOOK II

The Book of Parables

The second part of 1 Enoch is the Book of Parables (chapters 37-71). Although some scholars once dated this section of 1 Enoch as late as 270 CE, most now date the Book of Parables after 40 BCE and before 70 CE, based on a reference in 56:5 to an invasion by the Parthians, an ancient kingdom in what is now Iran. This means the Book of Parables was the last section of 1 Enoch that was written. The Book of Parables is the only one of the five sections of 1 Enoch missing from the Dead Sea Scrolls.

The date of the Parables is important because its writer uses the phrase "son of man." Jesus frequently uses this phrase to refer to himself in the Gospels. If the Book of Parables predates the Gospels, then this section of 1 Enoch may provide a context for reading the New Testament.

After a short introduction (chapter 37), the first parable (chapters 38-44) concerns the coming judgment, the second (chapters 45-57) concerns those who deny the name of the Lord, and the third (chapters 58-69) concerns the fate of the elect. The final two chapters of the Book of Parables describe Enoch's ascent to heaven.

The parables tell readers to expect a time of suffering for the righteous elect. Enemies will invade and trample the holy city. The righteous will be downcast and afflicted by the wicked. This time of suffering will end when the Righteous One (also called the Chosen or Elect One) sits on his glorious throne and judges the oppressors. The righteous will become like the light of the sun, and the days of their lives will be unending.

A key theme of the Book of Parables is the judgment of the wicked. When the Righteous One appears, sinners will be driven from the face

of the Earth (38:1) and melt like wax (52:6). The Elect One will judge the
fallen angel Azazel and all the rebellious watchers. The wicked will be
punished in a deep valley of burning fire and molten metal, where they
will be in chains with rough stones on their jaws.

THE FACTS AT A GLANCE

- The Book of Parables consists of three parables that
  describe a coming Chosen One who will judge the kings and
  mighty of this world, as well as the fallen angels.

- This section of 1 Enoch refers to a future resurrection of the
  dead. The dead will be judged and the righteous will live forever in the garden of life, but the wicked will be tormented
  in a fiery valley.

- Like other parts of 1 Enoch, this section makes a series of
  observations about the cosmos to show that the universe
  obeys God's wise commands.

- There are several fragments from a Noah legend inserted
  into the three parables. These may preserve parts of a lost
  Book of Noah.

- The third parable mentions two mythical creatures, Leviathan and Behemoth. The Old Testament book of Job
  describes the creatures in more detail, but like other early
  Jewish apocalypses, 1 Enoch says they will be destroyed at
  the end of this age.

- This section expands the list of names of the rebellious
  watchers, including five angelic beings with specific roles.

Section 8: Chapters 37–40

Novels and films sometimes set one scene as an homage to another. Kurt Vonnegut's *Cat's Cradle* begins with the words "Call me Jonah," alluding to the famous opening of the novel *Moby-Dick*. In *Toy Story 2*, Zurg tells Buzz Lightyear he is his father, referring to the iconic scene in *The Empire Strikes Back*. Similarly, the Book of Parables begins the same way the Book of the Watchers did, by introducing Enoch and establishing his credibility. In the Book of the Watchers, the author drew parallels between Enoch and Moses. The Book of Parables also claims God has given no one else the wisdom given to Enoch when he ascended to heaven. The Book of Parables contains this great wisdom.

Here are a few things to notice as you read this first section of the Book of Parables. First, there is a great deal of variation in the way the key characters are referred to. In the three parables, Enoch receives apocalyptic prophecies concerning the coming of a righteous judge who will punish sinners. In The Book of Parables, this coming judge is sometimes called the Righteous One, the Chosen or Elect One, the Son of Man, or the Lord's Anointed One or Messiah. Each of these titles draws on verses from the Old Testament and they all refer to the same messiah-like person. The author's community is called the righteous, the holy, or the chosen ones. God is called the Lord of Spirits, the Holy One, the Lord of Glory.

The Book of Parables also frequently refers to kings and the mighty who oppress the righteous in the land. The original readers of 1 Enoch in the first century CE would understand these powerful people as the Romans.

Second, keep in mind this is a Jewish apocalypse, so it contributes to a Jewish understanding of the messiah and a future messianic age—not one in which Jesus is the messiah. Early Judaism held a wide range of views on the messiah and his role in a future restoration of Israel. The Book of Parables looks forward to a figure anointed by God who will judge the nations that have been oppressing the Jewish people.

Third, also remember Christianity developed out of the Judaism of the first century, so there is language in these chapters that will be familiar to Christians. That Christians preserved and translated 1 Enoch shows they read these prophecies in a Christian context. Don't be surprised to read things in the Book of Parables that sound similar to the Christian apocalypse, the Book of Revelation.

KEY VERSES

"And in that place mine eyes saw the Elect One of righteousness and of faith, and righteousness shall prevail in his days, and the righteous and elect shall be without number before Him for ever and ever. And I saw his dwelling-place under the wings of the Lord of Spirits."

1 ENOCH 39:6–7

COMMENTARY

The Book of Parables begins by introducing Enoch as the recipient of great wisdom, given to him by the Holy One in the form of three parables. As you will see, these are not parables like Jesus's parables—simple stories to illustrate a spiritual truth. The Ethiopic word translated as "parable" reflects a Hebrew or Aramaic word that was associated with prophecy in the Old Testament. In the older King James (KJV) translation of Numbers 23:7, the prophet Balaam "took up his parable," but in the more recent New Revised Standard Version (NRSV) this is translated as "uttered an oracle." Isaiah 14:4 introduces a prophecy of the future destruction of the king of Babylon with this same word ("parable" in the KJV, "taunt" in the NRSV).

So, rather than simple stories, Enoch's parables are apocalyptic visions of the future.

How are these visions of the end of the age great wisdom? The Book of Parables speaks to the author's community, the chosen and righteous ones. The author offers comfort to those suffering in an evil world by sharing the secret knowledge God gave to Enoch: The salvation of the righteous is near, and so, too, is the punishment of the wicked.

The first parable begins in chapter 38 with the announcement that the time of judgment will begin when the "congregation of the righteous" appears. This phrase appears several times in the Book of Parables, and is like other descriptions of the righteous or faithful or godly in early Jewish literature, such as Psalms 149:1 and the book Psalms of Solomon from the first century BCE. The Qumran community (the community associated with the Dead Sea Scrolls) called themselves the "congregation of the chosen." In each case, the community considers itself to be the true people of Israel. When the last days finally come, God will rescue this righteous community from their oppressors.

The Righteous One will appear to judge sinners who have denied the Lord of Spirits and drive them from the face of the Earth. This anticipates the descriptions of punishment later in the Book of Parables. For those who denied the name of the Lord, it would have been better that they never were born. In Mark 14:21 Jesus used similar language to describe Judas as his betrayer: "It would be better for him if he had not been born." This time of judgment is when the secrets of the Righteous One will be revealed (38:3) and all the kings of the Earth will perish (38:5-6).

The second chapter of the first parable recalls the days when the rebellious watchers descended from heaven. Enoch is swept up to heaven in a whirlwind like the Old Testament prophet Elijah. He receives the "books of zeal and wrath, and books of disquiet and expulsion" (chapter 39). These books describe God's wrath against the watchers and sinful humans.

In another vision (chapter 39), Enoch sees the dwelling place of the holy ones in heaven who are interceding on behalf of humanity. These are humans who dwell with the righteous angels. In the same place, Enoch sees the "Elect One of Righteousness and of Faith."

In his vision, Enoch sees an uncountable gathering of angels (chapter 40). Among these angelic beings are four "who do not slumber." These are the obedient watchers introduced in 1 Enoch 20. In the Old Testament, there are cherubim near the throne of God (Ezekiel 1–2). In the New Testament, Revelation 4–5 describes four "living creatures surrounded by an innumerable crowd of beings standing in the presence of God." The unnamed angel who accompanies Enoch explains the names of the four angels:

- Michael, the merciful and forbearing
- Raphael, who is in charge of disease and wounds
- Gabriel, who is in charge of all power and strength
- Phanuel, who is in charge of those whose hope is eternal life

Unlike the Book of the Watchers, there are only four angels in this parable. We met three of them in 1 Enoch 20, but Phanuel replaces Sariel. The name Phanuel means "face of God," and he appears only on this list.

WHO IS the MESSIAH?

Popular media uses the word "messiah" to mean someone who thinks they are going to save the day. Sports
writers might call an outstanding basketball player like
Michael Jordan or LeBron James a messiah. Sometimes
news writers describe some politician as having a messiah
complex. But in the Old Testament, the word simply means
"anointed" and refers to someone chosen by God for a
task. For example, kings are called the Lord's anointed
because God called them to rule. A prophet literally
anointed the king with oil when he was made king.

In early Judaism, the word "messiah" was sometimes
used to describe the leader to whom God granted the
authority to rule over the nations. By the first century, many
Jews expected someone to come from God to conquer
the Romans, overthrow the priests in the Temple who
collaborated with them, and restore the Kingdom of God
in Jerusalem. The first-century Jewish historian Josephus
reports on several messianic pretenders who claimed
to work miracles and gathered a following. The Romans
executed these self-proclaimed messiahs for causing a
political disturbance.

The Gospels agree with Josephus that the Pharisees (a
first-century CE Jewish sect) were looking for the messiah.
In the New Testament, Luke 3:15 says crowds wondered
if John the Baptist was the messiah because "everyone
was expecting the messiah to come soon." The Pharisees
often questioned Jesus to see if he might be the messiah
(Matthew 22:41–45). When you read the New Testament,
it is sometimes helpful to change the word "Christ"
to "messiah," since the Greek word "christos" means
"anointed." "Christ" is Jesus's title, not his last name.

Section 9: Chapters 41–44

You may remember the 1980s documentary series *Cosmos*, written and hosted by Carl Sagan. Or perhaps you have seen the 2014 series hosted by astrophysicist Neil deGrasse Tyson. One theme in both series is that the universe follows an established set of laws. Scientists can know the exact movements of planets, comets, and stars by applying these laws. Ancient people made similar observations. They knew heavenly bodies followed predictable paths. In fact, for most ancient people, the universe was an orderly place.

Ancient Judaism considered the study of nature to be a form of wisdom. The creation story in Genesis narrates how God imposes order on the chaos of the primordial world. Proverbs 8:22–23 assert that God created wisdom at the beginning of his works. In this section of the Book of Parables, you will encounter a brief poem about wisdom and a description of the orderly universe obeying the laws of a wise God.

There are three themes in this second half of Enoch's first parable. First, just as God judged nations in the past, he is about to do so again. Kingdoms will be divided, and he will weigh the deeds of humanity. The agent of that judgment is the Chosen One. From the perspective of the writer, this future judgment will rescue the righteous from the hands of the powerful kings who have denied the Lord of Spirits.

Second, the author includes a short poem about wisdom trying to find a place to live in this world. The Old Testament book of Proverbs personifies wisdom and folly as women, each calling men to join them at their banquet. The wisdom book Sirach from the second century BCE also personified wisdom as a woman. In this poem, wisdom cannot find a place on Earth so she returns to heaven, but iniquity remains in the world.

The first parable ends with a series of astronomical observations—the third of the three themes. This is not modern science, but a theological statement about how God's wisdom runs the universe. Although these descriptions of natural phenomena seem strange to the modern reader, astronomical observations are common in the Old Testament and other early Jewish literature. Chronologically, this short poem reflects the theology of the Book of Astronomical Writings, which was written earlier than the Book of Parables.

KEY VERSES

"Wisdom found no place where she might dwell; Then a dwelling-place was assigned her in the heavens. Wisdom went forth to make her dwelling among the children of men, and found no dwelling-place: Wisdom returned to her place, And took her seat among the angels. And unrighteousness went forth from her chambers: Whom she sought not she found, and dwelt with them, as rain in a desert and dew on a thirsty land."

1 ENOCH 42:1–2

COMMENTARY

After seeing the four angels of the Lord of Spirits, Enoch saw all the secrets of heaven (chapter 41). The secrets God reveals to Enoch are "how the kingdom is divided and how human actions are weighed in the balance." Most scholars suggest an allusion to the "handwriting on the wall" in Daniel 5:26. Like Enoch, Daniel is a scribe who reads hidden wisdom written by the hand of God. For Daniel, the content of that wisdom is the impending fall of Belshazzar, the Babylonian king. In 1 Enoch 41, the kingdom about to be divided and weighed in the balance is the present oppressor of God's people, Rome. Later in the Book of the Parables, the Chosen One will judge the works of the holy ones by weighing them in a balance (61:8).

Enoch sees the dwelling place of the righteous. The older translation by Charles renders this "the mansions of the elect and the mansions of the holy," suggesting the presence of many mansions in heaven, as in a common mistranslation in John 14:2; modern translations (rightly) translate this as rooms or dwelling places.

Chapter 42 personifies Lady Wisdom as looking in vain for her place among the children of men. Since she can find no place among humans, she returns to live with the angels. Most scholars think this short poem is indebted to the Jewish book from the second century BCE, The Wisdom of Sirach. In Sirach 24, wisdom comes forth from the mouth of God and finds a place to live in Zion among the people of God. In Enoch's poem, there is no place for wisdom in this world, so she remains hidden in heaven. But when unrighteousness came out of her home, she found a place to live among humans. The poem concludes with a stunning metaphor: Iniquity is in the world like rain on a desert land. For the author of 1 Enoch, sin saturates this world and people are thirsty for it.

Why does a poem about wisdom appear in Enoch's first parable? Many scholars suggest the poem was misplaced and inserted into 1 Enoch in the copying process. However, it may be that this poem is a comment on the descent to Earth of the rebellious watchers and the obedient archangels. Only the rebellious angels find a place among humans, which results in the corruption of God's orderly creation.

The rest of the first parable is an astronomical text briefly describing the orderliness of God's creation. As in 1 Enoch 17–18, Enoch sees the cosmic storehouse for lightning, thunder, wind, and rain. He sees the place where the sun and moon begin their precise course through the heavens, as determined by God.

Many of these astronomical observations would be familiar to readers of the Old Testament. Job 38 describes God's heavenly storehouses for lightning and snow. Psalms 147:4 says God determines the number of stars and gives them their names.

LADY WISDOM

This section of 1 Enoch includes a poem personifying Wisdom and Iniquity as women looking for a place to live. Wisdom finds no home in this world and returns to heaven, while Iniquity makes her home among humanity. The Old Testament personifies wisdom as a woman, as well. In Proverbs 8–9 Lady Wisdom is calling out in the streets, inviting everyone to come and learn from her and find life. In Proverbs 9, Folly is also a woman inviting people to visit her home, although her guests end up in the depths of Sheol (the place of the dead). Some scholars suggest Lady Wisdom draws on the Egyptian goddess Maat because she is concerned with truth and the order of the universe.

The Wisdom of Sirach, which, dating from the second century BCE, is older than the Book of Parables, also begins by personifying wisdom as a woman. Following her leads to a blessed life and favor with the Lord (1:34–35). But Sirach 24 describes Lady Wisdom in more elevated terms: She came forth from the mouth of the Most High and was established in Zion, the dwelling place of God on Earth. Notice the contrast with 1 Enoch. In Sirach, wisdom left heaven and found a place, the Temple in Jerusalem, so that all who follow Jewish law will find God's wisdom.

In the apocryphal book Wisdom of Solomon (written between 50 BCE and 100 CE, about the same time as the Book of Parables), Lady Wisdom pervades all things and is the "breath of the power of God" and a spotless reflection of God's goodness (7:25). Wisdom reaches from one end of the Earth to the other and orders all things well. This helps explain 1 Enoch's frequent emphasis on the orderliness of the universe. It is God's wisdom that keeps the cosmos running well.

Section 10: Chapters 45–49

We like stories that end with justice and the hero living happily ever after. Good stories often involve a reversal of fortune, but in the end, everyone gets what they deserve. In the 1999 film *The Mummy*, Evie tells Beni (the bad guy), "You know, nasty little fellows such as yourself always get their comeuppance." I won't spoil the film for you, but when the story ends, the good guys are rewarded and the bad guys "get their comeuppance."

Like the first parable, this second one concerns a future judgment of those who deny the Lord of Spirits. It also tells the story of the great reversal of fortune at the end of the age. At a time of great tribulation, God names his judge, an anointed servant, the son of man, who will enter the world and judge the kings and nations who have been oppressing God's righteous people. There's a great reversal of fortune in which the righteous will enter a final kingdom, while the wicked will be punished. The details of that kingdom and punishment were hinted at earlier in the book and will be fleshed out in much more detail later, as well as in the rest of the Enoch literature.

Some scholars find this to be the most interesting section of the Book of Parables because of its similarities to parts of the Old Testament. It might be helpful to take a moment and read Daniel 7:14, Isaiah 49, and Psalms 2 to familiarize yourself with the Old Testament texts that this part of 1 Enoch draws on.

Although Enoch himself lives in the distant past, he is describing events at the end of time. The author of the book believes he is living near those end-times. He expects an anointed son of man to enter the world as God's judge, to rescue the righteous and punish the wicked.

KEY VERSES

"On that day Mine Elect Ones shall sit on the throne of glory and shall try their works, and their places of rest shall be innumerable."

1 ENOCH 45:3

"He shall be a staff to the righteous whereon to stay themselves and not fall, and he shall be the light of the Nations, and the hope of those who are troubled of heart."

1 ENOCH 48:4

COMMENTARY

The second parable begins with a description of the final judgment of the wicked and the vindication of the righteous. Those who deny the name of the Lord of Spirits will not ascend to heaven and will be kept for "the day of affliction and tribulation." On that day the Chosen One will "sit on the throne of glory" (45:3–4). Heaven and Earth will be transformed and the righteous will dwell on the new Earth.

In chapter 46 Enoch sees someone who has a "head of days." This being has the appearance of a man, his head is white like wool, and his face is full of grace "like the holy angels." Who is this person?

This description is similar to the mighty angel in Daniel 10:4-6, and also the description of Jesus in Revelation 1:12–16. Chronologically, the Book of Parables stands in between these two books, so both 1 Enoch and Revelation are, to some extent, dependent on Daniel. Scholars are divided on the identity of the angelic being in Daniel. He could be Michael or Gabriel—two angels mentioned in both Daniel and Enoch. The writer of the Book of Parables interprets the angelic being as the Chosen One who will judge the kings of the Earth. Revelation interprets the being in Daniel 10 as the resurrected and glorified Jesus.

The great reversal at the end of the age is a common theme in the Old Testament and early Judaism. In Daniel 7, a king will come who will speak words against the Most High, but eventually his kingdom will be abolished and dominion will be given to the holy ones of the Most High. In 1 Enoch, the Chosen One will remove kings from their comfortable seats and strong ones from their thrones, loosen the reins of the strong and crush the teeth of sinners (46:4). The faces of the strong will be slapped and they will be filled with shame and have no hope (46:6).

In the New Testament, John the Baptist describes the coming messianic age in terms of a settling of scores (Luke 3). Similarly, in Matthew 7:15–23 Jesus says that not all who are expected to be "in the kingdom" will be—even those who claim to do miracles in the Lord's name. While 1 Enoch clearly has the nations in mind, Jesus's idea of reversal seems to operate on a spiritual level: Those who think they are spiritually prepared for the kingdom may not be and may find themselves on the outside when the kingdom comes.

There is more in the second parable about the Chosen One drawn from the Old Testament. The Son of Man receives a name in the presence of the Lord of Spirits, but it is a name that was given to him from before the beginning of time. In other words, the Son of Man appears to preexist, since Enoch says he was chosen before the creation of the world (48:6). He will become a "staff for the righteous ones," and people may lean on him and not fall; he will be the hope of the lowly and needy and his name will be eternal (compare this to Psalm 72). As in Isaiah 42:6, he will be the light of the nations—meaning he will enlighten the nations, although it is not clear what this means. The righteous will be saved by his name (48:7).

How does this Son of Man relate to Jesus from the New Testament? Like the descriptions of Jesus, Enoch 48–49 describes the Son of Man by drawing from and combining messianic texts from the Old Testament. Although the Son of Man in 1 Enoch is ancient (maybe even existing before creation), he is different from God. But there is no indication that Enoch's Son of Man will suffer to accomplish his mission, as Jesus did.

Inserted into the description of the Chosen One is a prayer for the righteous (chapter 47). Enoch says the holy ones who dwell in heaven will unite to intercede on behalf of the righteous who have been killed. As a result of this prayer, Enoch sees the Head of Days seated on his throne with the books that will be used for judgment opened before him. As the righteous worship him, the Head of Days prepares to judge. In 48:1–2, Enoch sees the fountains of wisdom. Earlier, wisdom was searching for a place to dwell (chapter 42); now wisdom is pictured as a fountain in heaven to which all may come and drink.

Section 11: Chapters 50–57

A good fantasy story usually ends with an epic battle. The forces of evil line up on one side and the forces of good on the other, and they charge at each other one last time, with everything hanging in the balance. Enoch's second parable ends with a similar final battle. The kings of the Earth come from the east to trample the land of God's chosen ones. They are destroyed, and all creation worships the Lord of Spirits.

Here are some things to look for as you read the final pages of Enoch's second parable. First, for many readers, 1 Enoch 51 is one of the most important chapters in the book, since it refers to a future resurrection. Other than Daniel 12:1–2, there are few hints of a resurrection of the dead in the Old Testament. Second, this section of the Book of Parables describes the punishment of the wicked in more detail than earlier parts of 1 Enoch. Angels of punishment prepare the instruments of Satan, and the rebellious watcher Azazel is chained in the abyss.

OPENING *the* HEAVENLY BOOKS

Apocalyptic literature often describes the final judgment as a time when heavenly books are opened before a righteous judge. Both Daniel and Revelation describe tables full of books at the final judgment. This image is drawn from an ancient courtroom scene. Sometimes apocalyptic books record the names of the redeemed, but in many cases the books contain the names of the wicked to be erased from the books.

The Old Testament prophet Isaiah says the names of people destined to survive judgment have been "recorded for life in Jerusalem" (Isaiah 4:3). In the apocalyptic book 2 Baruch from the late first century CE, the opened books contain both the righteous deeds of the righteous and the wicked deeds of the wicked. These books are opened after a period of oppression, following which the messiah comes (2 Baruch 24–25).

In other apocalyptic texts, heavenly books contain hidden secrets God seals up to be revealed at the appropriate time. In Daniel 12:9-10 there are secrets sealed up "until the end of time." In the Book of Astronomical Writings, Enoch is given more secrets than he is permitted to write. In an expansion on the biblical story of Genesis, the Book of Jubilees from the first century BCE, Jacob is given seven tablets describing everything that will happen to his sons in the future (Jubilees 32:20-22).

In most judgment scenes, the heavenly books record the sins of the wicked being judged. 1 Enoch 90:14–22 includes an animal apocalypse, in which the names of the good and bad shepherds are carefully recorded in books for future judgment. In 1 Enoch 104:7, sins are investigated and "written down every day."

Third, Enoch's second parable ends with a description of an apocalyptic war that will trample the chosen ones. At the end of this war, Sheol will open its mouth and devour the dead.

In each of these three points, Christian readers may hear echoes of the Book of Revelation. Most scholars think the Book of Parables was written before Revelation, but they are not sure to what extent the writer of Revelation knew 1 Enoch. In both 1 Enoch and Revelation, the final battle results in mass casualties. In both, an evil angel is bound with chains in the abyss. Although there are many similarities, there are also important differences. For example, in Enoch's second parable the Chosen One does not fight in the last battle. In Revelation, the Messiah enters the final battle as a rider on a white horse who utterly slaughters his enemies. After reading this section of 1 Enoch, you may want to read Revelation 19:11–21 and 20:1–3 and compare and contrast these two apocalyptic texts.

KEY VERSES

"And in those days shall the earth also give back that which has been entrusted to it, and Sheol also shall give back that which it has received, and hell shall give back that which it owes. For in those days the Elect One shall arise, And he shall choose the righteous and holy from among them: For the day has drawn nigh that they should be saved."

1 ENOCH 51:1–2

COMMENTARY

The last section of Enoch's second parable is one of the most important sections of the Book of Parables for Christians, because it deals with the resurrection of the dead. In the end days, Sheol, the place of the dead, will give up all the dead and "my Chosen One" will sit on his throne and choose the holy ones out of the risen dead (51:1–2). After this resurrection, the "mountains will skip like rams" and the whole earth will rejoice (51:5). This is an allusion to Psalms 114:4. The context of that Psalm is a celebration of God's rescue of his people from Egypt, but the writer of 1 Enoch applies it to a future generation that will be similarly rescued.

The next two chapters describe Enoch's journey through a series of mountains made of various metals (iron, copper, silver, gold, a "colored metal," and lead). Some scholars suggest the author drew these metals from Daniel's vision of a statue representing four future kingdoms. If that is the case, these six mountains represent the kingdoms of the world. But it is also possible the mountains are the source of the wealth of the kings of the world who are about to be judged.

When the Elect One arrives, these mountains all melt like wax before fire and become like water at his feet. Several Old Testament prophets also describe mountains that will melt before the coming messiah, but in this case, the melting mountains represent the destruction of the earthly kingdoms.

Passing from the mountains, Enoch sees a deep valley filled with "gifts and tribute" brought by all the inhabitants of the Earth but the gifts cannot stop the coming judgment. Enoch sees angels of punishment preparing the "instruments of Satan," probably a reference to iron chains. These are not chains to bind Satan (as in Revelation 20:1–2)—rather, the angel with Enoch says the chains are being prepared for the kings of the Earth. The four archangels capture Azazel, the leader of the rebellious watchers, and throw him into the blazing furnace in the deep valley along with the kings of the Earth.

Most scholars consider 54:7–55:2 an insertion from a lost Book of Noah. The Book of Jubilees from the first century BCE describes Noah writing his visions in a book. There are some notable differences in this section that mark it out as separate from the rest of the Book of Parables. For example, God is called the Antecedent of Time (55:1). The paragraph has clear flood imagery (the waters above and below, the sign of the rainbow), which is absent in the rest of the second parable.

The last section of the second parable describes a great final battle. In 56:5–8 the angels will assemble against the Parthians and the Medes. This is a rare historical reference in 1 Enoch. As early as 247 BCE, the Parthians controlled an extensive empire that included the area of modern Iran. They were a constant threat to Rome's eastern borders and invaded Judea about 40 BCE. Many scholars use this invasion to date the Book of Parables after 40 BCE. The Medes were an ancient people who subdued the Parthians, but by the time the Book of Parables was written they had long since ceased to exist. Since the Medes joined Babylon to destroy Assyria and then later joined the Persians to capture Babylon, the writer may include them here as historical enemies coming from the east.

The Parthians are stirred to battle and overrun the land of the elect ones. But their army becomes confused when they get to the city of righteousness (Jerusalem) and attack one another. Armies that become confused and destroy themselves are not uncommon in the Old Testament—see Judges 7 and 1 Samuel 14. The Chosen One does not fight in the great battle. Instead, Sheol opens its mouth and swallows up the dead.

Section 12: Chapters 58–60

One of the most memorable moments in Christopher Nolan's *The Dark Knight* (2008) is Alfred's description of Batman's archenemy, the Joker: "Some men just want to watch the world burn." The Joker says his goal is to "introduce a little anarchy. Upset the established order, and everything becomes chaos. I'm an agent of chaos." Batman cannot predict what

RESURRECTION in the OLD TESTAMENT

The Old Testament is not clear about what happens when a person dies, and there are virtually no references to a future resurrection of the dead. In the earliest written parts of the Old Testament, people thought they went to the place of the dead, Sheol. There are only a few descriptions of Sheol in the Old Testament. It is a gloomy place deep in the Earth from which no one ever returns. Both the prophet Elijah and Elisha raise a dead person to life, but these are examples of resuscitations only a short time after the person has died.

One of the most significant Old Testament passages on resurrection is Ezekiel 37:1-14. In this vision, written after the Babylonian exile in 586 BCE, the prophet sees a vast valley filled with dry bones. God knits these bones back together and breathes his spirit into them, so they become living people again. However, this passage does not describe the personal resurrection of individuals, but the national resurrection of the kingdom of Judah. When the capital of Judah, Jerusalem, was destroyed, the nation went into exile. It was as if Judah had died. Only God can bring a dead nation back to life by restoring them from their exile.

In one of the last written texts in the Old Testament, Daniel 12:1-3 says that when the great prince Michael defends God's people, "many who sleep in the dust will awake, some to everlasting life, some to shame and everlasting contempt." Among the ones raised to everlasting life, "the wise shall shine like brightness in the sky above." This sounds enough like 1 Enoch 51:1 that many scholars suggest the author of 1 Enoch intentionally alludes to Daniel. Both envision a time when all the dead are raised, judged, and assigned to an eternal destiny (life or death).

the Joker will do because he makes little sense to Batman's well-ordered mind.

The third and last parable in the Book of Parables begins with a contrast between the chaos caused by the rebellious watchers and God's wise organization of creation. Like Batman and the Joker, order and chaos cannot exist in the same world. By the end of the Book of Parables, God will judge chaos, which came into the world through the fallen angels, and restore order to his universe.

Like the other two parables of Enoch, the third parable begins with a blessing on the righteous and chosen people. This is the author's community, and these words are meant to comfort them as they struggle in a world filled with darkness. When the final judgment comes, they will live in everlasting light, and darkness will be destroyed. Just as God destroyed the wickedness caused by the rebellious watchers, so, too, will he destroy the evil and chaos of the world in the author's time.

This section also contains another fragment of a Noah legend. As I suggested in the previous section, the story of Noah was integrated into the Book of Parables in various places. In the commentary here, I will treat the Noah legend separately. This helps preserve the flow of the third parable.

Finally, as you read this first section of the parable, be alert to the theme of chaos and order. This section mentions two mythical symbols of chaos, Leviathan and Behemoth. God's creation follows clear rules and patterns—unlike the chaos caused by evil.

KEY VERSES

"And on that day were two monsters parted, a female monster named Leviathan, to dwell in the abysses of the ocean over the fountains of the waters. But the male is named Behemoth, who occupied with his breast a waste wilderness

named Dûidâin, on the east of the garden where the elect
and righteous dwell, where my grandfather was taken up,
the seventh from Adam, the first man whom the Lord of
Spirits created."

1 ENOCH 60:7–8

COMMENTARY

Enoch's third parable begins with a blessing on the righteous and chosen. The righteous have a glorious destiny: They will live in the light of everlasting life and their days will be innumerable. This differs from the Book of the Watchers, where the righteous live long lives rather than everlasting life.

Most scholars rearrange the order of the verses to remove the Noah legend. After you finish reading chapter 59, skip ahead to 60:11–23. This part is like the previous heavenly tours in the Book of Parables and the Book of the Watchers, although there is more emphasis on interpreting the meaning of thunder and lightning. Sometimes thunder is a blessing, sometimes it is a curse. In the Greek and Roman world, thunder and lightning were omens that needed to be interpreted. Enoch receives the secrets of the thunder, but he does not tell his readers how to interpret these signs.

It is important to understand what the author of Enoch is saying about thunder and lightning. Most ancient cultures associated extreme weather with chaos myths. For example, the Canaanite god Baal is the rider on the storm who battles chaos. Enoch claims the wind, thunder, and lightning are not chaos at all, but part of God's orderly universe, and that the wise can learn the secrets of these phenomena.

There is a translation issue in this cosmology section. Enoch sees the place where the winds are divided and weighed. The Ethiopic word that is translated as "wind" can also mean "spirit." This is also true in Aramaic, the likely original language of the Book of Parables. It is therefore possible that the "weighing of spirits" refers to judgment. Most scholars think "wind" is the best translation here since the context is weather and other astronomical events.

Like the previous section of the Book of Parables, chapter 60:1–10 and 60:24–25 are part of a flood legend inserted into 1 Enoch. Scholars have known about this problem since the first publication of 1 Enoch. Although only a few manuscripts identify this specifically as Noah's vision, it must be Noah, since the writer dates the vision to the "year 500, in the seventh month, on the 14th day of the month in the life of Enoch." (The 14th day of the seventh month is the eve of Sukkot, when the Jewish people commemorate their journey in the wilderness after the Exodus from Egypt.) But Genesis 5:23 tells us Enoch lived only 365 years. Noah, on the other hand (who came three generations later), was five hundred years old when he fathered his three sons (Genesis 5:32). The next chapter in Genesis is the story of the sons of God and the daughters of men (6:1–4), so we can assume that happened right after Noah had his sons. Noah was six hundred years old when the Flood came (Genesis 7:6), implying that one hundred years elapsed between the rebellious watchers and the great flood.

Like Enoch in the Book of the Watchers, Noah is brought up to heaven, where he sees millions of angels and the Antecedent of Time sitting on a throne surrounded by glory. As is typical in apocalyptic vision literature, great fear strikes Noah senseless, and he cannot stand. Michael the archangel lifts him and strengthens him. Michael explains that the day of mercy has lasted until the present time, but now a day of punishment has arrived. In the context of Noah, the day of punishment refers to the great flood, but the author uses this ancient story to comment on his own time.

Another reason most scholars consider 60:7–10 and 60:24 to be misplaced fragments is because they describe two mythical monsters, Leviathan and Behemoth. The Old Testament book of Job describes the two creatures in detail. Two apocalyptic books of the late first century CE, 2 Baruch and 4 Ezra, preserve a tradition that God created these two beasts on the fifth day of creation to prepare for the time of the final judgment when God slaughters them to be used for food at the end days banquet.

The author of 1 Enoch describes Leviathan as a female creature living in the deep sea. Behemoth is a male who "holds an invisible desert in his chest." Recent translations render this a "trackless desert." This desert is called Dûidâin or Dunadayin—an unknown location. Early Enoch scholars suggested this was the land of Nod mentioned in Genesis 4:16, since it is east of the Garden of Eden.

Section 13: Chapters 61–64

On June 2, 1953, Queen Elizabeth II was crowned in Westminster Abbey. The coronation took fourteen months to prepare. It was the first coronation to be televised, and an estimated 277 million viewers were able to witness it. The procession route to Westminster Abbey was lined with thousands of guests and dignitaries. In her carriage, Elizabeth was accompanied by her mother, who was wearing a circlet crown set with the Koh-i-Noor diamond. Inside the church Elizabeth was surrounded by the most important people in the world. At the end of the ceremony, the crowds shouted, "God save Queen Elizabeth! Long live Queen Elizabeth! May the Queen live forever!"

As spectacular as this was, the coronation described in Enoch's third parable is even more so. The Lord of Spirits, God himself, seats the Chosen One, the Son of Man, on his glorious throne, where he will judge the nations who have oppressed the righteous and usher in a time of peace that will last forever.

WHAT ARE LEVIATHAN
and BEHEMOTH?

Leviathan is a sea serpent mentioned in ancient Canaanite mythology. It was a twisting, chaotic serpent with seven heads that is defeated by the god Baal. Scholars suggest Leviathan is the same as the chaos dragon, Tiamat, in the Babylonian creation myth. The god Marduk kills Tiamat and cuts her body in two, one part forming the sky and the other the Earth.

In the Old Testament, God battles Leviathan and destroys it (Isaiah 27:1). Referring to the events of the Exodus, Psalms 74:14 says God crushed the heads of Leviathan and gave him as food for creatures in the wilderness. The book of Job mentions both Leviathan and Behemoth. In God's second response to Job, he describes these two beasts to show his power over mythological chaos monsters. Behemoth is mentioned in Job 40. God commands and controls this terrifying beast, just as he does Leviathan. Most scholars think the author of Revelation modeled the seven-headed dragon in Revelation on the image of Leviathan, and it is possible the two beasts in Revelation 13 allude to Leviathan and Behemoth.

Although there is a great deal of speculation about what these creatures were, the important point for understanding 1 Enoch is that they are associated with a chaotic creation. God tamed the chaos of the primordial world by slaying Leviathan and taming Behemoth. One of the important themes of 1 Enoch's heavenly tours is that God's creation is orderly and there is no chaos.

As you read about this heavenly coronation, here are a few things to look for. First, pay attention to the guests who witness the enthronement of the Chosen One. I will have quite a bit to say about angelic beings in this chapter, because the glorious throne is surrounded by otherworldly beings. Because this section has much in common with Revelation, you might take a moment to read the enthronement scene in Revelation 4–5 along with this section of 1 Enoch.

Second, take note of the fate of the righteous and the wicked. Several times Enoch states that the righteous will live forever; their garments will not wear out nor will their glory fade. But the wicked will vanish from the presence of the Lord of Spirits, going down to the torments of Sheol. The torment of the wicked is a major theme later in 1 Enoch, as well as in 2 Enoch and 3 Enoch.

Third, there are some hints in this section about why the kings and the mighty are judged. For example, they confess to ill-gotten gain. They have possessed and ruled the land and harmed the Lord's chosen ones. Since the Book of Parables was written when Rome controlled Judea, it is likely the "kings and mighty" refers to the Roman empire. However, the landlords who used their power to oppress Enoch's community were likely local Jewish aristocrats.

KEY VERSE

"And the Lord of Spirits placed the Elect One on the throne of glory. And he shall judge all the works of the holy above in the heaven, and in the balance shall their deeds be weighed."

1 ENOCH 61:8

COMMENTARY

This section of Enoch's third parable begins with angels measuring the righteous with long ropes or cords. This is a method used to survey land in the ancient world. Later in the chapter Enoch says the righteous will live in the Garden of Life (61:12), so most scholars think the angels are measuring the Garden of Eden, the place prepared for the righteous. The wicked will be raised at the final judgment and will dwell in the depths of the Earth. In either case, no one will be destroyed.

After the garden is measured, the Lord of Spirits seats the Chosen One on his throne of glory and all the righteous worship the Lord of Spirits with one voice. In earlier sections of the book, Enoch described unimaginably huge crowds of angels and four archangels in the heavenly throne room (40:1–7). In this scene, there are three additional angelic beings (cherubim, seraphim, and ophanim) and "the angels of power and angels of dominion" (61:10). This heavenly court glorifies God with "the spirit of faith, and in the spirit of wisdom, and in the spirit of patience, and in the spirit of mercy, and in the spirit of judgment and of peace, and in the spirit of goodness" (61:11).

This scene may remind some readers of Revelation 4–5. John says he heard "the living creatures and the elders, the voice of many angels, numbering myriads of myriads and thousands of thousands" (Revelation 5:11). A key difference in Revelation is that the Lamb (Jesus) is regarded as equally worthy of worship as "him who sits on the throne." In 1 Enoch 61, the Chosen One joins the angelic host to worship the Lord of Spirits.

Now that the Chosen One is enthroned, Enoch turns to the fate of the kings and the mighty who oppressed the righteous. They are commanded to look upon the Chosen One, and pain comes upon them, like a woman in labor. They are terrified when they see the Son of Man sitting on his glorious throne. Readers of the New Testament may hear echoes of Jesus describing his future judgment of the nations: "When the Son of Man comes in his glory, and all the angels with him, then he will sit on his glorious throne" (Matthew 25:31). Even though the kings and the mighty fall down and worship the Son of Man, the wrath of the Lord of Spirits is on them, and they are commanded to depart from his presence (62:10). Those who are under the judgment of the Lord of Spirits worship the Lord and beg for mercy and confess what they have done (63:1–10). This long prayer by the judged seems to underscore the righteousness of the judgment against them.

Section 14: Chapters 65–71

Filmmakers like *The Sixth Sense* director M. Night Shyamalan are known for adding a twist at the end of their movies that shocks the viewer. When you get to the surprise ending, you can go back and rewatch the movie and notice all the plot points that led you to that final twist. But sometimes the ending is so unexpected that it raises more questions than answers. This is the situation at the end of the Book of Parables. After reading about the glorious enthronement of the Chosen One, the Son of Man who judges the kings of this world and raises the righteous ones to eternal life, the book ends with another section of a lost book of Noah and two appendixes that introduce some different ideas about Enoch.

Were chapters 70 and 71 originally part of the Book of Parables? The last line of chapter 69 is the end of the third parable, so it is possible chapter 70 and/or 71 was appended to the book later, before the collection known today as 1 Enoch was completed. The general consensus is that chapter 71 was not part of the original Book of Parables. The rest of Enoch's parables do not expect Enoch to be elevated to the Son of Man. Something similar happens in another Jewish apocalypse, the Testament of Abraham (usually dated to the second century CE).

CHERUBIM, SERAPHIM, and OPHANIM

When describing the heavenly room where the Lord of Spirits enthrones the Chosen One, Enoch mentions three angelic beings along with "angels of power" and "angels of dominion." Similar angelic creatures appear in Egyptian and Mesopotamian mythology. In the late Assyrian Empire, the lamassu were winged lions with human heads.

Of the three, cherubim are the best known from the Old Testament. God placed cherubim to guard the way back to the Garden of Eden and the Tree of Life (Genesis 3:24). Ezekiel 28 mentions an anointed guardian cherub on the holy mountain of God. The Tabernacle and the Ark of the Covenant were decorated with cherubim, and Solomon used images of cherubim inside the Temple and the Holy of Holies. The most detailed description of cherubim is in Ezekiel 1. The prophet describes four cherubim who guard the throne of God. They have four faces and four wings and are covered in eyes.

The seraphim are mentioned only in Isaiah's vision of the heavenly throne. These beings have six wings, and they are constantly worshipping the Lord with thunderous voices. Early Christianity thought of the seraphim as the most powerful angelic beings.

The Old Testament never mentions the ophanim, but the Dead Sea Scrolls mention them once, along with the cherubim, as guardians of God's throne. Since the name is related to the Hebrew word for wheels, the ophanim are associated with the throne of God in later Jewish mysticism, including 3 Enoch. Medieval Jewish mysticism developed a complex ranking of angelic beings. The twelfth-century Jewish scholar Maimonides thought the ophanim were the angels closest to God.

In that book, Adam is elevated to an almost God-like son of man.

Here are some things to look for as you read this last section of the Book of Parables. First, these chapters have more to say about the punishment of the wicked. The Enoch literature will develop this even further later, but in this section the condemned humans are sent to a great valley to suffer fiery tortures.

Second, this section has more to say about the rebellious angels introduced in the Book of the Watchers. Remember, the Book of Parables was written after the Book of the Watchers. How has the writer adapted the roles of the fallen angels to fit within his own historical context?

Finally, consider how this last section of the Book of Parables elevates Enoch from a prophet commissioned by God to the Son of Man himself. Is this a fitting conclusion to the book, or are scholars right in their assessment that the ending is from another source?

KEY VERSES

"And when all this took place, from that fiery molten metal and from the convulsion thereof in that place, there was produced a smell of sulphur, and it was connected with those waters, and that valley of the angels who had led astray (mankind) burned beneath that land. And through its valleys proceed streams of fire, where these angels are punished who had led astray those who dwell upon the earth."

1 ENOCH 67:6–7

COMMENTARY

Chapters 65–69 are other fragments containing traditions about Noah and the original judgment of the great flood. The story begins with Noah visiting his great-grandfather, Enoch, to complain about the wickedness in the world. Enoch responds by crying out sorrowfully and predicting the destruction of the world. In 65:6–12, Enoch describes the sins of the world, which have resulted in the coming deluge. Enoch then shows Noah the angels who have been prepared to cause the destruction of the Flood.

Noah is told by the Lord that the angels have constructed an ark to preserve Noah and his family so that they alone will survive the coming flood. God sends the Flood to imprison the fallen angels, although the floodwaters will also be a prison to the kings and princes of the world (67:8-9). These kings and princes are punished because they denied the "spirit of the Lord" (67:8, 10). Michael instructs Noah in the "secret things" that were written in Enoch's book (68:1).

Chapter 69 lists the names of the fallen angels as a conclusion to the Flood narrative. The twenty-one names listed in this section are nearly the same as in the list in the Book of the Watchers (6:7). Five rebellious watchers are called chiefs. Enoch gives a brief description of their roles.

- Yeqon: The name means "incited." This angel led other watchers to come to Earth (although in the Book of the Watchers Shemihazah led the rebellious watchers).

- Asbeel: His name means "deserter of God," although some scholars have suggested "May God arise." This angel advised the angels to ruin their bodies by joining with human women.

- Gadreel: The name means "wall of God," although some interpret it as "God is my helper." This is the angel who led

Eve astray and taught men to kill; he shows humans how to make weapons and armor, the instruments of death.

- Penemue: The name may mean "the inside," although it is not clear what it means. This angel taught men the secret wisdom of making paper and ink, causing men to sin "eternity to eternity and until this day."

- Kasdeya: Most scholars associate this name with Chaldean. The word itself refers to the neo-Babylon empire but was later associated with astrology. This angel taught humans "wicked smitings" and "flagellations of evil," including how to smite an embryo in the womb to kill it (abortion).

The angel Bîqâ (one of the faithful angels) has a hidden name that he reveals to Michael when he swears an oath (66:16–26). This secret oath describes all of creation as glorifying God and thanking him forever. The oath results in great joy because "that Son of Man" has been revealed. In verse 27 the Son of Man is described as eternal ("he will never pass away from the earth") and once again seated on a throne of glory in judgment.

Since the last line of chapter 69 is the end of the third parable, most scholars consider chapters 70–71 as an appendix to the Book of Parables. In this appendix, Enoch is taken to heaven in a chariot of winds, where he sees the patriarchs of old (70:4). His spirit continues to ascend until he is in the heaven of heavens (71:5). There he sees a structure made of crystals or hailstones with four sides, surrounded by living fire. He sees countless angels, including the four archangels, all worshipping the Head of Days. From this point on, there will be peace and righteousness (71:15–16).

In the final lines of the Book of Parables, we are told the chosen will dwell with "that son of man" who rules in the name of the Lord of Spirits forever. Who is this Son of Man? The four archangels and the Head of Days come to him and tell Enoch "You (are) that Son of

Man who was born for righteousness" (71:14). The rest of the Book of Parables implies the Son of Man and Enoch are two separate beings. Because of this, scholars often suggest 1 Enoch 71 comes from another source and was added to the Book of Parables at some point in the copying process.

Does this conclusion to the Book of Parables identify Enoch as the Son of Man, the Chosen One God enthroned to judge the nations? When Enoch first meets the Head of Days, he falls on his face, his flesh melts, and his spirit is transformed (71:11). After this transformation, he is told he is the Son of Man. Many scholars interpret these verses as commissioning Enoch as a prophet—but prepare for later Enoch literature to turn Enoch into an angelic being. In 3 Enoch 4, the angel Metatron, the prince of the divine presences with seventy names, identifies himself as Enoch, the son of Jared (as in Genesis 6:20).

WHAT'S WRONG with WRITING?

Modern readers of 1 Enoch might be surprised that one of the great evils the rebellious watchers introduced into the world is writing. In this section, Enoch says humans should not prove their trustworthiness through pen and ink. This is especially strange, since Enoch himself is a scribe and, at several times in 1 Enoch, he writes books. How can a written document condemn all written documents as evil? The author of the Book of Parables must have something else in mind.

In the Epistle of Enoch, Enoch warns his readers against those who "write lying words and words of error" because they lead people astray with lies (1 Enoch 98:15). It may be the case that the author of the Book of the Parables has in mind the kind of writing that leads people astray. There are many examples in the Old Testament of lying prophets leading people astray. The Dead Sea Scrolls condemn wicked teachers leading people astray with their lies. Jesus warns his followers to be on guard against false prophets who will lead many astray (Mark 13:6). The New Testament book of 1 John uses similar language to describe the work of false teachers.

Common to all these examples is that the speaker (or writer) claims to speak by the authority of God, yet from the perspective of a certain group, they are false prophets and lying teachers. It may be the case that Enoch's community saw literature produced by other groups as dangerous, since it led people away from Enoch's group.

BOOK III

The Book of Astronomical Writings

The Book of Astronomical Writings was written in Aramaic at the end of the third or the beginning of the second century BCE. Fragments of the book were found among the Dead Sea Scrolls but were not fully published until the 1980s. Scholars refer to the Ethiopic version as the Book of the Luminaries. This Ethiopic version is a translation of a Greek abbreviation of the Aramaic original. If this sounds too complicated, here's why it is important: Readers using translations of 1 Enoch published before the 1980s do not have access to the Aramaic fragments of the book. Some translators choose to work only with the Ethiopic text.

The Book of Astronomical Writings is a series of esoteric observations about the movements of the sun, moon, and stars. Everything in the book supports the use of a 364-day calendar (four seasons of ninety-one days each) rather than the 360-day calendar in use at the time. While this is an arcane and difficult section for the modern reader, the length of the year was a serious issue for early Jews because it has ramifications for keeping Sabbath, feast days, and Temple worship. If one celebrates Passover on the wrong date, does it count? The Qumran community (the community responsible for keeping the Dead Sea Scrolls) thought celebrating Passover on the wrong date was a sin, and they condemned the Jerusalem Temple for using a 360-day calendar.

In other words, the Book of Astronomical Writings presents a solar calendar for the purpose of setting holy days accurately. The Ethiopian Christian calendar is based on the Book of Astronomical Writings, although much of this evidence has still not been translated from Ethiopic. But there is nothing mystical about the calendar in 1 Enoch.

The Book of Astronomical Writings does not reveal "God's calendar" nor is it an apocalyptic road map for the future.

THE FACTS AT A GLANCE

- The Book of Astronomical Writings presents one of the earliest arguments for a 364-day calendar.

- Enoch's description of the sun, moon, and stars is based on the biblical creation story.

- Early Babylonian texts may have influenced the Book of Astronomical Writings.

- Enoch passes his secret astronomical knowledge on to his son Methuselah.

- In the last days, God's orderly creation will become chaotic.

Section 15: Chapters 72–76

My favorite part of basic science class in elementary school was learning about the solar system. Maps of the solar system fascinated, me and I loved learning about the planets. I remember having a chart that listed the length of a year on each planet, and how much you would weigh if you lived there. I even won a blue ribbon at the science fair for my model of the solar system.

Like my first introduction to science, this new section of 1 Enoch is about the laws of the heavenly bodies. Although quite different from a modern astronomy lesson, the Book of Astronomical Writings describes the movements of the sun, moon, and stars. In some ways its arguments are (almost) accurate, since the book concludes that a year is 364 days. But the writer reflects the ancient world's view of the universe.

Here are some things to watch for as you journey through the cosmos with Enoch. First, the Book of Astronomical Writings assumes the biblical creation story is fact. In Genesis, God created the sun, moon, and stars "to be signs for seasons, days, and years" (Genesis 1:14). This differs from other ancient cultures, which often considered the sun, moon, and stars to be gods.

Second, laws of nature don't change. The seasons follow set patterns and rules that will not change as long as the Earth remains (Genesis 8:22). Psalms 148:5–6 say God decreed that the sun, moon, and stars will never pass away. The second-century Jewish wisdom book Sirach agrees that God has arranged an "eternal order" (16:26–28). The idea that creation is unchanging is at the heart of 1 Enoch as well.

Third, you might think you've read these things before in 1 Enoch. This is true. Because the Book of Astronomical Writings is the earliest part of the collection, it influenced later sections. For example, in 1 Enoch 33–36, Uriel guided Enoch through a series of gates at the ends of the Earth. Most scholars think the author of the Book of the Watchers knew the Book of Astronomical Writings and used it as a model for Enoch's heavenly journey.

KEY VERSE

"The Book of the courses of the luminaries of the heaven, the relations of each, according to their classes, their dominion and their seasons, according to their names and places of origin, and according to their months, which Uriel, the holy angel, who was with me, who is their guide, showed me; and he showed me all their laws exactly as they are, and how it is with regard to all the years of the world and unto eternity, till the new creation is accomplished which endureth till eternity."

1 ENOCH 72:1

COMMENTARY

The Book of Astronomical Writings introduces the angel Uriel (the name means "God is my light/fire"), and claims this most important of the angels revealed the information about the movement of the sun, moon, and stars to Enoch. Several times, Enoch writes down the information Uriel reveals.

The introduction also claims the rules revealed in this book will remain "until the new creation is accomplished." In other words, the present creation will pass away, but the new creation endures forever. The idea of a new creation is based on Isaiah 65:17 and 66:22. In those passages, the prophet looks forward to a time when creation will be restored to the conditions of the Garden of Eden. Revelation 21 also describes a new heaven and a new Earth.

But there is no final judgment or messianic judge in the Book of Astronomical Writings. The writer is only interested in charting the movement of the sun and moon to correctly determine the length of the year.

The Book of Astronomical Writings is the earliest evidence for a Jewish 364-day calendar. Ancient Mesopotamian culture used a lunisolar calendar with twelve months of twenty-nine or thirty days. This is like the modern Jewish calendar and the lunisolar calendar used in Islam. The Old Testament does not explicitly favor a lunar calendar, but by the time the Book of Astronomical Writings was written, the length of the year was controversial. 1 Enoch 75 is clear: A 364-day year is God's design and anyone using a different calendar is in error.

There is one additional problem to consider. The Book of Astronomical Writings argues the 364-day calendar is part of God's perfect creation, but the year is short by a day and a quarter every year. After just a few years, the seasons do not line up with the actual length of a solar year (365.24 days). The Gregorian calendar (used in the West since 1582) solves the problem with a 365-day calendar and a leap day every fourth February.

In 1 Enoch, the sun, moon, and stars emerge from heavenly gates in the east, pass through the sky, and exit through gates in the west. Although Mesopotamian myth also describes the sun entering and exiting the sky through a heavenly gate, the Book of Astronomical Writings says there are six gates in the east and six in the west. The gates represent months; the sun passes through each twice over the course of a year. In the first month of the year, the sun passes through the fourth gate and travels for thirty days. This results in a thirty-day month—except months three, six, nine, and twelve, which are thirty-one days. The solar year is therefore 364 days. The moon moves between the gates more quickly, spending as few as one day and as many as eight days at each gate. Each lunar month has either twenty-nine or thirty days and the lunar year is 354 days.

Section 16: Chapters 77–82

Americans traveling in the Middle East encounter a different calendar. For Americans, the weekend is Saturday and Sunday. But in Israel, Friday is preparation for the Sabbath, and people go back to work on Sunday. In Islam, Friday is the special day of worship, so some Arab countries consider Thursday and Friday as the weekend and return to work on Saturday. If you are planning on visiting people, you need to know when the "weekend" is for them.

The Book of Astronomical Writings deals with a similar problem, but it is far more complex because it is trying to show through astronomical observation that the calendar should follow a solar year, not a lunar year. There are four seasons of thirteen weeks each; fifty-two weeks or 364 days in the year. The righteous, the book concludes, will not walk like the sinners who follow the wrong calendar.

The first part of this section (chapters 77–79) concludes with Enoch's astronomical observations. The rest covers two additions

THE BOOK of JUBILEES and the BOOK of ASTRONOMICAL WRITINGS

The Book of Jubilees is an anonymous Jewish book from the second century BCE summarizing the book of Genesis and Exodus 1–12. Like the Book of Astronomical Writings, many fragments of Jubilees were found among the Dead Sea Scrolls. Jubilees likely drew on the Book of Astronomical Writings, since it also argues in favor of a 364-day year.

The writer of Jubilees claims Enoch was the first person who learned writing and knowledge and wisdom, and he "wrote in a book the signs of the heaven according to the order of their months, so that the sons of man might know the (appointed) times of the year according to their order, with respect to each of their months" (Jubilees 4:17). Following the wrong calendar is dangerous, it says, because God's people will forget the feasts of the covenant.

Although Jubilees argues for a 364-day calendar, it never discusses the length of months. A major difference from the Book of Astronomical Writings is that Jubilees is mainly interested in the dates for festivals and other sacred days. the Book of Astronomical Writings says those who use the wrong calendar are sinners, but never connects the calendar to Temple worship.

In fact, 1 Enoch, Jubilees, and the Dead Sea Scrolls all consider using a 354-day calendar spiritually dangerous. So, who was using the wrong calendar? When the Book of Astronomical Writings was written, virtually everyone, including the priests at the Temple. Both the Book of Astronomical Writings and Jubilees warn their readers against "walking in the feasts of the gentiles" by arranging the liturgical calendar incorrectly.

to the Book of Astronomical Writings. In chapter 80, Uriel reveals the coming destruction in the last days, which will reverse the order of the sun, moon, and stars. In chapter 81, Enoch passes his knowledge on to his son Methuselah and warns him about the seriousness of using the wrong calendar.

Here are a few things to focus on as you read this section. First, when you read Enoch's description of geography in chapter 77, is it possible to identify the seven mountains or seven rivers? If this is sacred geography, what is at the center of the map?

Second, although the Book of Astronomical Writings has far less to say about the end-times than other sections of 1 Enoch, Uriel's speech in chapter 80 is significant. It draws on some key Old Testament texts to describe a time in the future when God's orderly creation will become chaotic.

Third, the last few chapters of the Book of Astronomical Writings introduce Enoch's son, Methuselah. Even less is said about Methuselah in Genesis than in Enoch—other than mentioning his very long life. But his grandson Noah is very important in the biblical story, so some traditions developed about the righteousness of Methuselah. This section of 1 Enoch is the earliest reference to these traditions.

KEY VERSES

"I have given wisdom to thee and to thy children, and thy children that shall be to thee, that they may give it to their children for generations. This wisdom (namely) that passeth their thought. And those who understand it shall not sleep, but shall listen with the ear that they may learn this wisdom, and it shall please those that eat thereof better than good food."

1 ENOCH 82:2–3

COMMENTARY

Chapters 77–79 continue Enoch's observations about the seasons. Ancient astronomical texts often include geographical notes on the four directions. Enoch says the first quarter is the east, the second is the south. In the Ethiopic text, Enoch adds that the "Most High will descend" in the south, but the Aramaic text from the Dead Sea Scrolls (dating to the second century BCE) says the second quarter is called south because "there the Great One lives forever." (The difference is likely the result of a mistranslation. Remember, the early English translations relied only on the Ethiopic manuscripts and did not have access to the earlier Aramaic fragments.) The third quarter is called "diminished" since that is the direction in which the sun sets. The fourth quarter is the north, the place where humans live, but the garden of righteousness is there as well.

Enoch 78 gives two names for the sun. Earlier scholars suggested the first name, Aryares, meant "my light is the sun." More recent interpreters suggest the name reflects a Hebrew word for the sun ("heres," in Greek "ares"). The second name, Tomas, is related to a Hebrew word for heat. The two names may reflect two seasons: a cooler and a warmer part of the year. The moon has four names: Asanya, Abla, Banase, and Era. Although it is possible these names are related to words associated with the moon or possibly the phases of the moon, it is impossible to know their exact meaning as they passed from Aramaic, through Greek, and into Ethiopic.

Chapter 79 is the conclusion to the Book of Astronomical Writing since many scholars suggest 1 Enoch 80–82 were later additions. There are some important differences that support this conclusion, such as the use of Enoch's name for the first time in chapter 80. Chapter 80 describes a time in the future when the sun will stand still, the seasons will grow shorter, the fruit of the Earth will not come at the normal time, and the moon will change its order. Even the stars will change their course. Such conditions will cause drought and famine.

Enoch says he has shown all these things to his son, Methuselah. Since Enoch mentions Methuselah several more times in chapters 81–82, this is a good place to consider some traditions about him. The only thing most people remember about Enoch's son, Methuselah, is that he lived longer than anyone else in the Old Testament—according to Genesis 5:27, he lived 969 years. This means he died in his grandson Noah's six hundredth year, the year the Flood began. Because of this, some have considered Methuselah's name to be a prophecy of the great flood. In some Rabbinic traditions, Methuselah was a righteous prophet who to tried to turn the generation wiped out by the Flood back to God. Later (in 1 Enoch 108), Methuselah receives secret books from Enoch.

In Chapter 81, Uriel tells Enoch to read from the tablets of heaven and to report this information to his son Methuselah. These heavenly books contain all that will happen when the judgment of the great flood comes. Enoch passes this knowledge on to his son in chapter 82. The wise will listen closely to these words, which are more pleasing than fine food.

The Book of Astronomical Writings then ends with an explicit statement that the true year ought to be 364 days (82:4–6). The computations that Enoch learned are true, the book concludes, because they were communicated to him by the angel Uriel himself.

MESOPOTAMIAN INFLUENCES
on ENOCH

Although the book is anonymous, it may be possible to trace some of the writer's influences. For some Enoch scholars, the author of the Book of Astronomical Writings knew the work of Calippus, an ancient Greek astronomer who worked with Aristotle in the early 300s BCE. He observed thirty-four cycles of heavenly bodies and measured the four seasons. However, more recent studies reject this since the idea of four seasons is not uniquely Greek.

It is more likely the author of the Book of Astronomical Writings was influenced by Mesopotamian astronomy. Scholars often point out parallels between Enmeduranki, the seventh king in the Sumerian king lists. Like Enoch, he lived before the great flood and was taken to heaven to learn the secrets of the sun and stars.

The most likely Mesopotamian text to have influenced the writer of Enoch is an astronomical text known as MUL.APIN, or the Plow Star. Although the two cuneiform tablets date to 686 BCE, scholars suggest it was first compiled about 1000 BCE. Like the Book of Astronomical Writings, this ancient text traces the path of the stars and how many days the sun follows its path. It is the basis of Babylonian astrology.

Because of these similarities, scholars suggest the Book of Astronomical Writings was written by Jews living in Babylon. Since 586 BCE, Jews lived in Babylon and many adopted and/or influenced Babylonian culture. In the Old Testament, Nebuchadnezzar made the Jewish captive Daniel "chief of the magicians, enchanters, Chaldeans, and diviners" in Babylon. There are many other Jews who served the powerful in Babylon and Persia, so it is likely they knew the calendar from tablets like the Plow Star.

BOOK IV

The Book of Dream Visions

In the Book of Dream Visions, Enoch tells his son Methuselah about two dream visions he had when he was a young man. In the first vision he foresees the destruction of the world in the great flood. As a result of this terrifying vision, he cries out to the Lord in prayer and begs God to leave a remnant alive and not destroy all humanity. This prayer of intercession is the reason God preserves Enoch's great-grandson Noah and his family in the great flood.

Enoch's second dream is known as the Animal Apocalypse. This is an allegory of Israel's history up to the time of the Maccabean Revolt (164–160 BCE). Most of the elements of the allegory will be familiar to readers of the Old Testament. For example, the sheep in the vision represent Israel. They often go astray and are attacked by wild beasts. Israel is often described as sheep in the Old Testament as well (Psalms 95:7), and they went astray by worshipping idols. As punishment, God allowed one or another national group to oppress his people. This pattern is common in the Old Testament and is repeated several times in the Animal Apocalypse.

Since this part of Enoch makes a clear reference to Judah Maccabee, the leader of the Maccabean Revolt, most scholars date the book after 160 BCE, the year Judah was killed in battle. But it is possible the Animal Apocalypse was written as early as 200 BCE and the vision was updated to include the Maccabean Revolt.

Like other visions in the Enoch books, the author of this section is really talking about religious and social issues in his own day. Everything in the dream visions leads up to the Maccabean Revolt and looks forward to a future restoration of God's people and the renovation of the Temple.

THE FACTS AT A GLANCE

- ♫ Enoch's first dream is a vision of the destruction of the Earth in the great flood—an event in the distant past by the time the book was written.

- ♫ Enoch describes the great flood as a return of primordial chaos.

- ♫ God saves Noah and his family in response to Enoch's prayer.

- ♫ Enoch's second dream is an allegory of Israel's history from creation to the final judgment.

- ♫ The second dream is called the Animal Apocalypse because it uses various animals to describe the flow of Israel's history.

- ♫ The Animal Apocalypse shares some imagery with the book of Daniel.

- ♫ In the Animal Apocalypse, the Lord of the Sheep sits on his throne to judge the sheep and the shepherds—the people and the leaders of Israel.

Section 17: Chapters 83–84

People of a certain generation remember when they first heard the news about the attack on Pearl Harbor. A later generation remembers where they were when they heard President John F. Kennedy was assassinated. For my generation, we remember the moment we first heard about the 9/11 terrorist attacks. I remember someone told me what happened, then I went home early to watch the news reports. I remember seeing people devastated and weeping uncontrollably. Like most, it was difficult to speak about what I saw. The first vision in the Book of Dream Visions affects Enoch similarly. He sees the coming flood that will destroy the world and all life on Earth. His only response is to cry out to God.

Like the Book of Astronomical Writings, the Book of Dream Visions begins with Enoch passing on his secret knowledge to his son Methuselah. Enoch says he received these visions before he was married and was still living with his grandfather, Mahalalel ("God is shining"). In the first vision, Enoch sees the destruction of the coming flood. Although it takes up only a few verses, Enoch is terrified by the dream. His grandfather Mahalalel asks him why he is crying out.

Since this is Enoch's first vision, he requires guidance from his grandfather to understand it and respond to the Lord properly. Perhaps recalling the Old Testament story of young Samuel's first prophetic message, the elder Mahalalel tells young Enoch how to respond. Enoch passes this on to his own son, Methuselah, who will die the same year the Flood comes.

There are a few things to watch for as you read these two chapters. First, the Flood is described as a chaotic destruction of creation. The Book of Astronomical Writings focused on the orderliness of creation, but the Book of Dream Visions begins with the undoing of that order. After his vision Enoch cries out, "The Earth has been destroyed!"

Second, Enoch's response to the vision is prayer. The theme of this prayer is God's lordship over creation. As you read, notice all the ways Enoch describes God's power. Since God is all-powerful and eternal, he can destroy the Earth because of the sins of the angels. But he can also preserve Enoch's descendants when he devastates the Earth.

Third, Enoch's request for God to preserve a righteous remnant is also an important theme drawn from the Old Testament. No matter how bad things were in the Old Testament, there was always a righteous remnant who remained faithful to God's covenant. In this vision, the righteous remnant is very small. Among the humans, God preserves only Noah and his family when the Earth is destroyed.

KEY VERSES

"I saw in a vision how the heaven collapsed and was borne off and fell to the earth. And when it fell to the earth I saw how the earth was swallowed up in a great abyss, and mountains were suspended on mountains, and hills sank down on hills, and high trees were rent from their stems, and hurled down and sunk in the abyss."

1 ENOCH 83:3–4

COMMENTARY

Enoch received his first vision before he was married. Genesis 5:21 says he fathered Methuselah when he was sixty-five years old, so we may not think he was young, but here in 1 Enoch 83 he is young enough to need the guidance of his grandfather. The vision is brief, but powerful: Heaven was thrown down to Earth, and Earth was swallowed by the great abyss. Mountains and hills collapsed, and everything sank into the abyss. This is a flood of apocalyptic proportions that is able to sweep heaven and Earth into a pit so deep that nothing remains. The vision refers to the outpouring of God's wrath on the world because of the rebellious watchers.

To fully appreciate this vision of the coming flood, we need to read it in the context of Genesis 1. When God created the heavens and the earth, the earth was "formless and void and darkness was over the face of the deep" (Genesis 1:2). The phrase "formless and void" suggests the pre-creation world was complete chaos, without any order or purpose. The word used in the original Hebrew for "the deep" can refer to primordial waters, and the Greek translation from the second century BCE used the word "abyss." Although the word can refer to the depths of the ocean, it often refers to the underworld.

In the biblical creation story, God gives order and function to the chaotic waters so that his creation is well-designed and functions as he intended. He separates the heavens from the dry land and the sea and populates them with appropriate plants and animals. This theme of the orderliness of creation is the basis for the Book of Astronomical Writings and several other sections of 1 Enoch.

What Enoch sees in this first vision is the complete undoing of creation. When he is finally able to speak, all Enoch can do is cry out, "The Earth is destroyed!"

After he explains his vision to his grandfather, Mahalalel tells him the burden of sin is so great that the Earth must sink into the abyss. But there is a possibility God will allow a remnant to remain. He therefore counsels Enoch to pray for the Earth (83:6–9), which he does (83:10-11, 84:1-6).

Enoch goes outside and sees the sun, moon, and stars and is reminded of God's creation. He begins his prayer by praising "the Lord of Judgment" and acknowledging his sovereignty (83:2–4). This prayer is remarkably similar to Isaiah 66:1–2. Like the prophet Isaiah, Enoch says God's throne is in heaven and he uses the Earth as his footstool. Like Daniel 7:14, God rules over all creation and his majesty and power will never end.

After praising God, Enoch makes a request on behalf of the current generation. Even if the angels must be judged, Enoch prays that God will allow a remnant of humans to survive the devastation. He asks God to raise up the righteous and true "as a seed-bearing plant" (84:6). In the context of the biblical flood story, this refers to Noah and his family. Noah is the only righteous man left, and his family is saved to repopulate the world.

At the time the Book of Dream Visions was written, the final judgment was still in the future. The author of Enoch wants God to preserve a righteous remnant in the coming apocalyptic judgment, just as he preserved Noah at the time of the great flood.

Section 18: Chapters 85-90

You may have read George Orwell's famous allegorical novel *Animal Farm*. In this story, farm animals stage a revolution, run the farmer out, and establish a new government where "all animals are equal." As the story progresses, though, the pigs take more control, and eventually, "All animals are equal, but some animals are more equal than others." If you read that story literally, it makes very little sense. But when you realize it is an allegory of the Russian Revolution and the rise of Stalinism, it makes perfect sense.

Enoch's second dream is the Animal Apocalypse, a remarkable allegory of Israel's history from Eden through the Maccabean Revolt. The first part of the Animal Apocalypse presents Judah Maccabee as the legitimate successor to biblical heroes like Moses and Joshua, men the "Lord of the Sheep" empowered to lead the people. Some scholars suggest the allegory was written early in the Maccabean period as propaganda to support Judah's actions. But the Lord of the Sheep did not intervene in the apocalyptic judgment described in 90:20-27, which does not refer to a historical event in the Maccabean period. Like the detailed prophecy in Daniel 11, the history is accurate only up to the point where the author speculates about a future intervention by God to restore Israel.

The animal imagery is based on Ezekiel 34 (sheep and shepherds) and the frequent use of sheep imagery in Psalms (95:6-7, for example). In the earliest part of the dream vision, who and what the various animals represent is obvious, but as the allegory becomes more detailed, it is more difficult to determine what the original writer had in mind. For example, 1 Enoch 89:2-9 obviously refers to the great flood. An angel teaches the white cow how to

A RIGHTEOUS REMNANT

The first of Enoch's dreams reflects an important theme of the original flood story: Even in the darkest times, God preserves a righteous remnant. The idea of a righteous remnant is found throughout the Old Testament. During the ministry of the prophet Isaiah in the eighth century BCE, the Assyrian Empire threatened to annihilate Jerusalem. But God promised Isaiah that even if everything is destroyed, there will still be a holy seed that remains. In fact, Isaiah named his son Shear-jashub ("a remnant will return") as a sign that God would preserve a righteous remnant of his people.

After Jerusalem was destroyed in 586 BCE and the Babylonians exiled many Jews, the prophets still identified a small righteous remnant that would return to Jerusalem after the time of judgment was over. Writing in about 520 BCE, the prophet Zechariah looked forward to when the righteous remnant would return from the east and west to live in Jerusalem in peace and prosperity (Zechariah 8:1-13).

By the first century BCE, the community that wrote the Dead Sea Scrolls thought of themselves as the righteous remnant. According to the War Scroll, a book produced by the community, they thought God guarded them as a remnant of true Israel in the present evil world. When the messiah comes, he will rescue their community and judge the rest of the world.

The Book of Dream Visions stands within this tradition. In the biblical story, the righteous remnant is Noah and his family. But the author believes his own community is the righteous remnant of true Israel. Like Enoch after his first dream vision, the author prays to God to preserve his community as a righteous remnant of true Israel.

build an ark and then the cow becomes human and builds it. But in 90:6, a generation of deaf and blind white lambs are born. This likely refers to some of the Jewish people who had returned to Jerusalem after the Babylonian exile, but exactly which group the author had in mind is not clear.

Here are some things to think about as you read through the Animal Apocalypse. First, you may want to review the book of Daniel after you read the Animal Apocalypse. Daniel 9:24–27 also describes Israel's history as seventy "weeks of years" (490 years total). Daniel 8 describes Persia and Greece as a ram and a goat. Daniel 11 contains a detailed prophecy about Judea in the Persian and Greek periods.

Second, if you have some familiarity with the Old Testament, try to work out what the Animal Apocalypse is alluding to. I will make some suggestions, but it is impossible to cover every detail in this chapter.

Third, pay attention to the description of final judgment and the future new age at the end of the Animal Apocalypse. In some ways, this part of the vision is like the Book of Parables, but there are some important differences.

KEY VERSES

"And I saw till a throne was erected in the pleasant land, and the Lord of the sheep sat Himself thereon, and the other took the sealed books and opened those books before the Lord of the sheep. And the Lord called those men the seven first white ones, and commanded that they should bring before Him, beginning with the first star which led the way, all the stars whose privy members were like those of horses, and they brought them all before Him."

1 ENOCH 90:20–21

COMMENTARY

The Animal Apocalypse begins and ends with Eden. Enoch sees a white bull and a heifer (Adam and Eve) to whom two bulls were born, one black and the other red. The black bull (Cain) gores the red one (Abel), killing it. The heifer comes after the black bull, but the white bull quiets her and she gives him another white bull (Seth)—a reference to the purity of the line of Seth—along with many other bulls and black cows.

The Animal Apocalypse then traces the history of the pre-flood world. Stars mingle with the cows, giving birth to elephants, camels, and donkeys. The cattle become frightened and they bite and gore one another, referring to the rebellious watchers from 1 Enoch 6–11. In 1 Enoch 87 a snow-white person comes down from heaven and rescues Enoch from the chaos and tells him to watch the elephants and other animals. Four heavenly beings seize the fallen stars and imprison them in the abyss.

1 Enoch 89:10–27 summarizes the rest of Genesis and Exodus. Israel is a sheep surrounded by wolves. The Lord of the Sheep rescues the sheep and then leads them out of a swamp and into the desert. In the desert, the Lord of the Sheep opens the eyes of the sheep (89:28–38). One of the sheep is the leader, becomes a man, and is taken up into heaven—an obvious reference to Moses. The sheep are led across a stream (the Jordan River) to a "pleasant and glorious land" where they live in peace (Joshua). When the sheep become dim-sighted, another sheep is appointed to lead them. Their eyes open again, but a variety of animals oppress the sheep (Judges). The kings of Israel are rams. Solomon is a "little ram" who built a house (the Temple) for the Lord of the Sheep (89:50).

After briefly passing over the kingdom of David, 89:51–67 offers significant details for the divided kingdom after Solomon. In 89:59, seventy shepherds are summoned and commanded to watch over the sheep. These shepherds are responsible for what the sheep do, implying these are the seventy elders or priesthood of Israel (Exodus 24:1). Scholars vigorously debate the identity of these seventy shepherds. For many, the seventy were angels, since they received their orders from God, and humans are animals in the Animal Apocalypse. But a few key characters in the allegory are human. Noah, for example, was a bull who became human when given the commission to build the ark.

1 Enoch 89:68–72 briefly narrates the exile of Israel. The sheep are delivered to oppressors, and many are killed. Verse 72 is the return from exile and the rebuilding of Jerusalem and the Temple under Ezra and Nehemiah. In 89:73–77, the city and Temple are rebuilt, but the sheep are weak and poor-sighted (the post-exile community in Israel).

The apocalypse becomes more detailed in the Maccabean period (90:6–12). A "great horn" grows on one lamb, and it rallies the sheep against the oppressors—likely a reference to Judah Maccabee. In 90:13–19, the sheep (Israel) battle the beasts. The Lord of the Sheep intervenes in wrath; he strikes the ground with his rod and gives a great sword to the sheep to kill the beasts of the Earth.

Beginning in 90:20–27, the Animal Apocalypse shifts to the future. A great throne is set up in the pleasant land (Israel). The Lord of the Sheep, who struck the Earth with his rod, sits upon the throne to judge the sheep and the shepherds. Like the Book of Parables, books are opened, and the Lord of the Sheep punishes seven shepherds for killing more sheep than permitted. These shepherds are cast into the fiery abyss. The rest of the seventy shepherds are found guilty and also thrown into the abyss.

The Lord of the Sheep then renovates the old house (the Temple, or the city of Jerusalem) into a new, greater, more beautiful house (90:28–36). There are many traditions about a new Jerusalem in both the Old Testament (Ezekiel 40–48) and the New Testament (Revelation 21:1–4). Enoch's vision is a prophecy of a restored Temple of Solomon. In this new age, the sheep are white and their wool is "thick and pure" (90:32). For the first time, there is "none among them who do not see" (90:35).

Finally, in 90:37–38 a new snow-white bull is born with huge horns. All the sheep and other animals of the world fear this new bull. He transforms all the animals into white cows, not stopping until they are all transformed. This snow-white bull is the future good shepherd who will care for God's people properly.

The messianic figure is not a sheep (like David and Solomon), but a bull. This is a new Adam or Seth, the last characters in the apocalypse to be described as bulls. Even if the reference is to Seth, this bull is a "son of Adam," or "son of man," a title for the messiah in the Book of Parables. All the animals are transformed into snow-white cattle. This is an unexpected universalism: In the new age, all the nations will worship the God of Israel.

VATICINIA EX EVENTU

Every year, the Procrastinators' Club celebrates National Procrastination Week by releasing their predictions for the year to the press. Unlike most lists of predictions, the Procrastinators' Club does not get around to making their predictions until March of the next year. As a result, their predictions are always 100 percent accurate.

This is the situation in 1 Enoch. The Animal Apocalypse claims to be written by Enoch, a prophet who lived long before the Flood. But in fact, it was written before 160 BCE, after almost everything in the dream vision had already happened. Scholars consider the Animal Apocalypse to be an example of *vaticinia ex eventu*, a Latin phrase that means "prophecy from the event." There are examples of this practice in Greek and Roman literature. For example, Virgil's *Aeneid* (written 29–19 BCE) tells the story of a hero from the Trojan War (which happened in the twelfth or thirteenth century BCE), and "predicts" the rise of Augustus, who would rule Rome and usher in a golden age. Many scholars consider Daniel 11 an example of *vaticinia ex eventu*, accurately predicting the course of history from the Persian period to the Maccabean Revolt.

Why would the writer of the Book of Dream Visions use *vaticinia ex eventu*? Since the allegory leads up to Judah Maccabee, the great horn who opens the eyes of the sheep (90:9–10), it appears the author intended the Animal Apocalypse to support the Maccabean Revolt. Although the allegory is generally accurate up to the time of Judah, the author obviously gets things wrong. The final judgment does not take place, the Lord of the Sheep does not sit on his throne and judge the wicked sheep, nor is the old house replaced with a new one. Beginning in 90:20, the author shifts from *vaticinia ex eventu* to genuinely predicting the end of the age.

BOOK V

The Epistle of Enoch

1 Enoch 91–108 is usually titled the Epistle of Enoch, although the contents include the allegorical Apocalypse of Weeks and a series of speeches on ethical issues. The final three chapters of 1 Enoch were added as appendixes. They discuss the birth of Noah and Enoch's last words to Methuselah.

Most of this section is in the form of a last testament. Enoch reflects Old Testament ethics by warning his children that there are only two paths: the way of righteous (which leads to life) and the way of iniquity (which leads to judgment and death). A last testament was a popular literary style in early Judaism and was based on Jacob's final words in Genesis 49. In the second century BCE, writers produced many such last testaments attributed to the patriarchs or other important Old Testament characters. Like the Epistle of Enoch, these last testaments addressed ethical and social issues that were important at the time they were written.

Most readers are interested in the Apocalypse of Weeks, a summary of history from creation to the end of the world using the metaphor of ten weeks. Although not as detailed as the Animal Apocalypse, this section looks forward to the time when God purges evil from the world. Something to watch for: 1 Enoch 91:12–17 was misplaced in the copying process. These verses describe the eighth and ninth weeks, but in the incorrect copies, chapter 93 ended with the seventh week. Most modern editions of 1 Enoch rearrange the text so that the weeks are in order, but some leave the weeks out of order without any explanation.

THE FACTS AT A GLANCE

- The Epistle of Enoch is more like Jewish wisdom literature than apocalyptic literature.

- The Epistle of Enoch assures the righteous they will be rewarded in heaven, even if they suffer in this life.

- The Apocalypse of Weeks describes history in ten periods that the writer calls "weeks."

- The writer of the Apocalypse of Weeks believes he is living in the seventh week, a time when a wicked generation arises. This may allude to the events leading to the Maccabean Revolt.

- This section preserves legends about the miraculous birth of Noah. The child is so strange that his father, Lamech, assumes Noah's real father was one of the rebellious watchers.

Section 19: Chapters 91–93

In recent American history, there have been several failed attempts to predict the end of the world or the beginning of the end-times. Perhaps you remember the Y2K bug that was going to plunge the world into darkness on January 1, 2000. American Christian radio broadcaster Harold Camping predicted the rapture of Christians and the beginning of the great tribulation on May 21, 2011 (later pushed back to October 21). There were many predictions of the end of the world on December 21, 2012, based on the Mayan calendar.

These predictions of the end of the world are not new. Jewish, Christian, and secular writers have calculated and recalculated the end many times over the past two thousand years. These incorrect predictions of the end of the world as we know it are based on a particular understanding of scripture and history. Like the author of this section of 1 Enoch, many of these doomsayers see the present word as completely corrupt. God must judge it, as he did leading up to the original flood. After wiping out the wicked, the righteous (usually the predictor's followers) will enter paradise.

The Apocalypse of Weeks gives the same general outline of the future as the Book of Parables and the Book of Dream Visions. All history leads to a future judgment of the wicked, including the rebellious watchers responsible for sin entering God's creation in the Book of the Watchers. After this judgment, the righteous will live forever in an ideal, sinless world. Although this apocalypse does not suggest a date for the coming judgment, the author alludes to historical events in the recent past to suggest God is about to put an end to wickedness, as he did in Noah's time.

Here are a few things to think about as you read this section. First, as you read the Apocalypse of Weeks, consider how the original audience might have understood the prediction of the imminent judgment of the wicked. What did the author want his readers to do after hearing this prophecy? Would this prophecy comfort them? Did the author want to motivate his readers to godly living?

Second, consider how the author of the Apocalypse of Weeks uses the language of the Old Testament and applies it to his vision of the future vindication of the righteous. For example, Isaiah's "new heaven and new earth" becomes an eternal life of righteousness.

Third, if you are not familiar with the Maccabean Revolt, you may want to take some time to learn about that period in history. In the Apocrypha, 1–2 Maccabees relates the history of the period from two different perspectives (see the Resources).

KEY VERSES

"There shall be the great eternal judgment, in which He will execute vengeance amongst the angels. And the first heaven shall depart and pass away, and a new heaven shall appear, and all the powers of the heavens shall give sevenfold light."

1 ENOCH 91:15–16

COMMENTARY

In the introduction to the Epistle, Enoch tells the reader they should not be troubled by difficult times because the Holy and Great One has declared "specific days for all things" (92:2). The Righteous One will wake from his sleep and walk in righteousness forever. God will give the Righteous One authority to judge. The righteous will "walk in eternal light," while the "sin and darkness will perish forever." As in the Book of Parables, Enoch looks forward to a messianic age when God appoints a Righteous One to establish God's rule on Earth and judge justly.

The Apocalypse of Weeks is a vision concerning the sons of righteousness. Like the other sections of 1 Enoch, this introduction establishes Enoch's authority as one who has seen and read secret knowledge in heaven. It says the righteous watchers gave Enoch this vision of the future and he learned everything from reading heavenly tablets (93:2). This secret knowledge summarizes history, beginning with Enoch, through the great flood, and up to the present time of the writer. Israel's history is divided into ten periods of history, called "weeks." These periods are not evenly distributed chronologically; the first few weeks cover thousands of years. As the writer gets closer to his own time, the week covers fewer years.

The first six weeks are easy to summarize.

- ❧ The First Week (93:3): Enoch was born in the first week, a time when "righteousness endured."

- ❧ The Second Week (93:4): After Enoch's time, great and evil things arise and the first destruction of creation takes place—the great flood. Only Noah survives the Flood. But the Flood does not eliminate sin, so God creates a law for sinners, that "whoever sheds the blood of man, by man shall his blood be shed" (Genesis 9:6).

- ❧ The Third Week (93:5): God chooses a man as a "plant of righteousness" and a second man as an "eternal plant of righteousness." The first is Abraham, the second is Moses.

- ❧ The Fourth Week (93:6): Visions of old and righteous ones will be seen and "a law will be established as a fence." This refers to the Law of Moses.

- ❧ The Fifth Week (93:7): "A house and a kingdom" are completed—the establishment of the kingdom of David.

- ❧ The Sixth Week (93:8): At the end of the week, the house and kingdom will be burned, people will be blindfolded, and the "chosen root" dispersed. This is the period from King David to the fall of Jerusalem (586 BCE) and the Babylonian Exile.

In the seventh week (93:9–10) a wicked and perverse generation will rise. Near the end of this time, "the chosen will be chosen." Since this week refers to the events during the exile, most scholars associate the perverse deeds with the events leading up to the Maccabean Revolt. The true high priest was deposed and eventually murdered. Two Jewish men, Jason and Menelaus, bribed the Seleucid King Antiochus so they would be named to the high priesthood. But there is no obvious reference to the Maccabean Revolt or Judah Maccabee. We know the seventh week is when the author of the Apocalypse of Weeks lived, since the next three weeks describe the future eternal kingdom of righteousness.

Based on parallels to the Book of Parables and the Apocalypse of the Animals, the seventh week should have ended with a messiah figure seated on a glorious throne judging the nations. Scholars have made several suggestions to solve this problem. Most of these solutions are complicated theories that rearrange the text. For example, 1 Enoch 92:3-5 can be moved to the end of the seventh week. This is entirely possible, since all scholars recognize that 91:11-17 is the conclusion of the Apocalypse of Weeks.

The final three weeks describe the judgment of the wicked and the vindication of the righteous. The eighth week is a time of righteousness when a glorious and eternal temple of the Great One will be built (91:12-13). In the ninth week (91:14), all the deeds of wickedness will vanish from the Earth. Finally, in the tenth week, the rebellious watchers will be judged, and the old heaven will pass away. A new heaven will appear and "the powers of heaven will shine eternally sevenfold." After the ten weeks, there will be a time of "many weeks which number forever" when righteousness will never end and sin will never be mentioned again (91:17).

Section 20: Chapters 94-99

How do you live a successful life? A quick search of Amazon yields hundreds of books promising to teach you the habits of successful people. Many books promise to teach you to become a happier and more thankful person. Who doesn't want those things? The problem is a book does not guarantee success or happiness. You can adopt all the habits of successful people and your business can still fail.

HISTORICAL PERIODS

Ancient writers often divided history into periods—just as modern historians do. The Greek poet Hesiod (sixth century BCE) divided history into four periods (gold, silver, bronze, and iron), from the heroic age to his present time.

Christians sometimes divided biblical history into six ages based on the six days of creation. 2 Peter says, "With the Lord a day is like a thousand years, and a thousand years are like a day." Some say this suggests that since there were six days of creation before the Sabbath, human history is divided into six ages with a future one thousand years of rest. The Mishnah (a record of the oral law that was transmitted after the destruction of the second Temple in 70 CE) and the Talmud (the rabbinic law that expands on the Mishnah) have a similar scheme, although the dates are based on the Jewish calendar.

Like Hesiod, the book of Daniel uses metals to depict the progress of empires from Babylon to the writer's own time. Like the Apocalypse of Weeks, Daniel also uses the metaphor of a "week of years," or a seven-year period. In Daniel 9:27, the angel Gabriel tells Daniel there are "seventy weeks as decreed for your people," meaning, "490 years are decreed." After the first 483 years, the "anointed one will be cut off and have nothing." Some interpreters of Daniel see this as leading up to the Maccabean Revolt. Many Christian scholars calculate the years as predicting the coming of Jesus as the messiah.

The Apocalypse of Weeks is somewhat like these Jewish and Christian conceptions of history, although it offers no attempt at a precise chronology. Unlike Daniel, the "second week" is not seven years, but the hundreds of years between the life of Enoch and Noah. And the third week runs from the Flood to the time of Moses—nearly one thousand years.

In the Old Testament and early Judaism, wisdom literature taught the art of successful living. If a person lived out the life described in Proverbs, they would be happy or successful. At least that was the promise. The book of Job is about one of the wisest, most righteous people who has ever lived, yet he suffered horribly. Like biblical wisdom literature, this section of 1 Enoch describes how to live a wise, righteous life, but also responds to the question about the suffering of the righteous in this life.

This section of the Epistle of Enoch contains six speeches describing a wise and righteous life that leads to blessing, in contrast to an unrighteous life that leads to judgment. For convenience, I will cover the first three speeches in this section and the second three in the following section.

1. Woe Against Injustice (94:6–96:3)

2. Woe Against the Rich (96:4–98:8)

3. Woe Against False Religion (98:9–99:10)

4. Woe Against Lawlessness (99:11–100:6)

5. God's Justice Is Certain (100:7–102:3)

6. God's Judgment of the Living and the Dead (102:4–104:8)

As you read the first three speeches in this section, here are some things to think about. First, the biblical book of Proverbs and the wisdom book Sirach from the second century BCE express similar ideas. For example, Proverbs 17:13, Sirach 12:7, and 1 Enoch 95:5 all warn against repaying evil with evil. Jesus also expressed this idea (Matthew 5:39), and it appears later in the New Testament (Romans 12:17, 1 Peter 3:17).

Second, notice how many of the issues Enoch raises in these speeches concern social issues. The Old Testament prophets frequently condemned the leaders of Israel for their abuse of the poor, widows, orphans, and immigrants. Although Jewish wisdom literature never condemned riches, it often condemned the rich for their treatment of the poor. Similar themes appear in the teaching of Jesus (Luke 6:21–26) and the New Testament letter of James (5:1–6).

Third, the Epistle of Enoch is an example of Old Testament "two ways theology." The Law of Moses ends with a promise of blessing for those who keep the law, but a promise of woe for those who do not keep the law. Keeping the law leads to life, but breaking the law leads to death. In Proverbs, one either is wise or foolish: wisdom leads to life; folly leads to death. The clearest statement of two ways theology is Psalm 1. Take a moment to read this short psalm before reading the Epistle of Enoch.

KEY VERSES

"Woe to you, ye sinners, who live on the mid ocean and on the dry land, whose remembrance is evil against you. Woe to you who acquire silver and gold in unrighteousness and say: 'We have become rich with riches and have possessions; And have acquired everything we have desired.'"

1 ENOCH 97:7–8

COMMENTARY

The final chapters of 1 Enoch are advice to his children and follow a pattern not unlike the Old Testament wisdom literature. Often, Proverbs presents wisdom as wise advice from a father to his son. As I suggested in the introduction to the Epistle of Enoch, the model for this section is a last testament. Like Jacob in Genesis 49, Enoch gathers his children to pass on his wisdom and encourage them toward righteous living.

Enoch begins by using a familiar metaphor drawn from the Old Testament (94:1–5). He tells his children there are two paths: the path of righteousness, which leads to peace, prosperity, and life, and the path of iniquity, which leads to violence and death.

So, imagine Enoch on his death bed with his children gathered around him. The six speeches are his last words to them, encouraging them to live a righteous life.

The first woe is against people who build wealth through iniquity and violence. The rich are deceitful and build up luxurious households by oppressing the poor. This is a common theme among the Old Testament prophets. The prophet Amos of the eighth century BCE condemned the wealthy in his day for trampling the needy through economic oppression (Amos 8:4–6). Micah is another prophet from the eighth century BCE who vividly described the leaders of Israel as hating good and cling- ing to evil as they oppress the poor. Enoch encourages his own righteous community by assuring them the sinners will perish. In contrast to the wealthy, the ones who have suffered will receive healing (96:3). This is a hint that Enoch's community was on the losing end of society and saw the wealthy aristocracy as abusive.

In the second woe, Enoch continues to condemn the rich and mighty who oppress the righteous. They may eat and drink the best foods now, but when the Day of Judgment comes, they will be put to shame. Christian readers may remember Jesus made similar contrasts in the Beatitudes (Matthew 5:3–12). The prayers of the oppressed will come to the Lord, but not so the prayers of the sinners. Instead of prayers, their lawless deeds will be revealed before the Great Holy One and he will put the oppressors to shame (97:4–6).

The third woe begins with a warning to the fool because they do not listen to the words of the wise. In Jewish wisdom literature, a fool is not ignorant, but is someone who knows the truth and willfully ignores it to pursue wickedness. This section contains more graphic descriptions of sin. For example, the wicked drink blood, a practice forbidden by Jewish law. They write lying words that lead others astray, possibly a reference to false prophecy. All this evil causes bitterness on the Earth and arouses God's wrath.

Enoch ends the third speech with a final encouragement to the readers. Like Psalm 1, blessed is the person who listens to these wise words and walks in the path of righteousness. The one who is traveling the path of righteousness will be saved.

Section 21: Chapters 100–104

In the popular TV show *The Good Place*, Eleanor Shellstrop dies and suddenly finds herself in "the good place" as a reward for her exemplary moral life. The good place is an ideal town populated by exceptionally good people who experience all kinds of wonderful things as a reward for their righteous lives. The problem is neither Eleanor nor her friends were exceptionally moral in life, and they actually deserve to be in "the bad place."

I will not spoil *The Good Place* for you, so let me just observe that the idea of heaven as a good place where people are rewarded with physical pleasure for living a good and moral life is indebted more to books like 1 Enoch than to the Bible. Certainly, there are some hints in the Bible about heaven and hell, but 1 Enoch begins the development of the "good place" and a "bad place" as they have appeared for centuries.

This section of the Epistle of Enoch asks about the rewards for living a good life. Do people who lived a righteous and pious life really end up better off than the wicked rich who abused the poor? Is there any advantage to living a righteous life? Enoch has read the secret tablets in heaven and can assure his readers that the righteous will indeed enjoy good things in the presence of the Great One.

Here are a few things to watch for as you read the moral exhortations in the second half of the Epistle of Enoch. First,

WOE!

The Epistle of Enoch uses the word "woe" frequently. In both Hebrew and Greek, the word sounds as if one is making an exasperated, mournful sound (onomatopoeia). Although in English the word expresses pain or unhappiness, in both the Old and New Testament, the word is associated with prophetic judgment. This includes judgment on Israel's enemies or on Israel itself.

Isaiah 5:8–21 uses the word in a way that is quite similar to this section of 1 Enoch. Isaiah was prophet from the eighth century BCE who announced God's judgment on his people because they had broken the covenant. Rather than list a series of religious offenses, Isaiah announced six woes on the rich and powerful members of Jerusalem's aristocracy. Because they have made themselves rich through falsehoods and lies, Isaiah said, the nobility of Jerusalem will go down to Sheol, the place of the dead.

Early Jewish apocalyptic literature regularly used the word "woe" when announcing the imminent judgment of a nation. The third Sibylline Oracle (an apocalyptic book from the second century BCE) announces woe on many of the enemies of Israel (Babylon, Egypt, Greece). The apocalypse 4 Ezra from the late first century CE describes the time of tribulation as "messianic woes."

Jesus uses woe in the New Testament in a similar way. In the Gospel of Matthew, Jesus pronounces woe on villages that rejected him as the messiah (Matthew 11:20) and the hypocrites who claimed to the follow the law but did not (Matthew 23). In Luke 6:20–26, Jesus blesses the poor but pronounces woe on the wealthy.

notice the contrast between the righteous and the wicked. For the writer of the Epistle of Enoch, there are two paths: one leading to righteousness and another leading to wickedness. It's either one or the other, and one must choose one's path in this life.

Second, in the last two speeches in the Epistle of Enoch the righteous and the wicked face the final judgment. For the righteous, final judgment is nothing to fear. Even though both the righteous and the wicked die and go to the place of the dead, the righteous will be raised to a good place where they will be rewarded for their earthly labors. The wicked will also be raised, but they will be in a place of darkness and distress for all eternity. Although 1 Enoch only briefly describes these eternal rewards and punishments, later books, including 3 Enoch and Dante's *Divine Comedy*, expand and develop what kinds of rewards and punishments await us when we die.

KEY VERSES

"And, although ye sinners say: 'All our sins shall not be searched out and written down,' nevertheless they shall write down all your sins every day. And now I show unto you that light and darkness, day and night, see all your sin."

1 ENOCH 104:7–8

COMMENTARY

Like the first three sections of the Epistle of Enoch, the fourth speech (99:11–100:6) begins with a series of woe statements condemning those who have built their wealth through lawlessness. The wicked have built their houses on a foundation of deceit and "all their building materials are the bricks and stones of sin" (99:12).

Following this, there is a vivid description of the Day of Judgment awaiting the wicked. Fathers, sons, and brothers will slaughter one another until their blood flows like a river. A horse and chariot will wade through this bloody river. The same metaphor appears in the Book of Revelation: Blood will flow as high as a horse's bridle for about 184 miles (Revelation 14:20). When the Most High executes judgment, he will send angels to protect the righteous and holy, and they will live in peace. Enoch tells the reader to contemplate the words of his book so that they can avoid this hellish judgment.

The fifth speech in the Epistle of Enoch is different from the first four. Although 1 Enoch 100:7–102:3 begins with a series of woes, it is like another type of Jewish wisdom literature, the book of Job. In the biblical story, Job is a righteous man who suffers so horribly that his friends conclude God is punishing him for his sins. But Job insists he has not sinned and calls on God to explain his justice. When God finally speaks, he does not tell Job the reasons for his suffering. He simply describes his sovereign power over the universe because he is the creator. Similarly, Enoch invites the readers to contemplate the work of the Most High. As in 1 Enoch 2–5, here Enoch asks a series of rhetorical questions about nature that are intended to show God's sovereign control of the universe. If God is in control of nature, then he is worthy to judge humanity.

In the last speech in the Epistle of Enoch (102:4–104:8) the author is answering a question about God's justice in the present world. The previous speeches agree God will judge the wicked in the future, but what about the lack of justice for the righteous in the present world? In 103:9–15, the righteous complain that they have lived a pious life but the lawless ones crushed and destroyed them. When they complained to their rulers, there was no response. In fact, the rulers strengthened the lawless ones and never punished their sins.

Enoch says he has read the secret tablets in heaven that describe the fate of the righteous. Enoch calls this knowledge a mystery. This word refers to something that remains hidden and unknowable until it is revealed. In this life, the righteous do not know what God has planned for them in heaven. All Enoch says here is that God prepared good things for the righteous who have died and that they will live forever. But the sinners who have accumulated sinful wealth and prosperity will go down to Sheol in great distress (103:4–5). They have already had their easy life, so their souls will endure heavy judgment for all eternity.

The author of the Epistle of Enoch comforts his own community, who are suffering from oppression by the wealthy aristocracy. God has heard their cry and he will reward them. Although the sinners think their deeds will never be discovered, Enoch promises that God will expose their abuse of the poor righteous ones, and they will be judged. The righteous should, therefore, take courage. Even though they have been worn out in this life, at the coming judgment they will shine like the stars and heaven will be opened to them. The righteous should have no fear of the coming judgment (104:1–6).

In the conclusion of the Epistle of Enoch, the writer once again tells the readers to pay careful attention to the words of this book. The righteous (who will be blessed in the coming judgment) will learn the path of truth by reading Enoch's book.

Section 22: Chapters 105–108

Hollywood has produced many movies featuring a precocious child who is far more intelligent than the average child. Some are based on true stories, like *Searching for Bobby Fischer* (1993); others are complete fantasy, such as *Baby Geniuses* (1999) or *Look Who's Talking* (1989). Although entertaining, there would be something terrifying about a newborn child standing up and talking like an adult.

In this final section of 1 Enoch, you will read the unnerving story of the birth of Noah. When his father, Lamech, first sees him, he is terrified by the infant's appearance. From the

APOCALYPTIC BLOOD and GORE

One of the most disturbing elements of apocalyptic literature is the image of horrific slaughter on the Day of Judgment. Because modern readers think of God in terms of love and mercy, they react strongly to the descriptions in the Old Testament of God as a warrior. It might shock them to read Exodus 15:3-4, "the Lord is a man of war." Isaiah 63:1-6 describes the Lord as a warrior treading on his enemies like grapes, staining his robe with their blood. There are several Jewish sources that combine the imagery in Isaiah 63 and Exodus 15 to describe the coming messiah as a warrior.

This way of depicting power and judgment is consistent with the rest of the ancient Near East. Egyptian art often depicted the Pharaoh slaughtering his enemies. Mesopotamian kings living at the time of Isaiah boasted about slaughtering their enemies and decorated their palaces with battle scenes depicting torture. Read in the context of ancient Near Eastern culture, all these verses describe God as the ultimate king who will violently judge his enemies.

Written in the sixth century BCE, Ezekiel 39:17-20 is likely the source of the blood and gore in apocalypses like 1 Enoch and Revelation. Like a scene from an Assyrian or Babylonian battle, when the final judgment comes, birds and animals will gorge themselves on the flesh and blood of God's enemies.

So did the author of the Epistle of Enoch think the final judgment would produce a literal stream of blood as deep as a horse's breast? Although some interpret apocalyptic slaughter in a literal sense, it may be the case that these images of blood and gore are a metaphor for the ultimate victory of the greatest king, God himself.

moment of his birth, Noah can talk. Although we are familiar with the authors of 1 Enoch embellishing the life of Enoch, there is nothing to prepare us for Noah the wonder baby!

Here are a few things to consider as you read these final chapters of 1 Enoch. First, when you read the legend of Noah's birth, consider how the writer describes baby Noah. Some descriptions are like the angelic being in Daniel 10 or John's vision of Jesus in Revelation 1. The writer of this section intentionally describes Noah as an angelic or semidivine being.

Second, although some readers might be tempted to draw parallels between Noah's miracle birth and Jesus's virgin birth, the two stories have little in common. Although the Gospels of Matthew and Luke are clear that Jesus's mother, Mary, was a virgin when she conceived him, there is nothing miraculous about the actual birth, nor is the child described as anything other than a normal child. Noah's mother is not a virgin, but the baby is very unusual.

Third, since the last chapter of 1 Enoch was intended as a summary of the book, think about why this summary focuses on the things it does. For example, despite reading about the punishment of the rebellious watchers in virtually every section of the book, the final chapter does not mention them. The summary is more interested in the judgment of humans. Why do you think this is the case?

KEY VERSES

"And I will bring forth in shining light those who have loved My holy name, and I will seat each on the throne of his honour. And they shall be resplendent for times without number; for righteousness is the judgment of God; for to the faithful He will give faithfulness in the habitation of upright paths."

1 ENOCH 108:12–13

COMMENTARY

The final chapters of 1 Enoch are fragments of other documents appended to the main text. The first section is a legend about the birth of Noah. When Noah is born, his body is whiter than snow and redder than roses; his hair is snow white and curly like wool. His eyes glow like the sun and when he opens them, they light up the entire house. As soon as he was born, he stood up and praised the Lord. His father, Lamech, is upset by this odd child, suspecting an angel fathered the baby. Lamech goes to his father, Methuselah, for advice, but Methuselah sends him to Enoch, who predicts the Flood as a judgment for sin.

Enoch also predicts Noah and his family will be the remnant in the great judgment to come. Enoch alludes to the sins of rebellious watchers. These predictions are confirmed because they were written on heavenly tablets (107:1–2). Enoch confirms the child is Lamech's and tells him to name the boy Noah. The child will be righteous and blameless, Enoch says, and his family will be saved from the judgment of the great flood.

The final chapter of 1 Enoch was written for Enoch's son, Methuselah. Enoch tells his son that those who observe the law ought to wait patiently (108:1–3). He describes a vision of an invisible burning cloud that is explained by an angel as the place where sinners go (108:4–7). Those who love God endure. Although they suffer in the body, God will make recompense for what they have suffered (108:8–10). The righteous who endure will eventually see the end of those who are unrighteous (108:11–15).

Scholars think this final chapter was added to the collection as a summary and interpretation of 1 Enoch. The coming judgment will separate the righteous from the wicked. The righteous will live in glory, each seated on a throne of honor where they will shine forever. The wicked will be slaughtered and thrown in a fiery place of severe torment.

LEGENDS ABOUT the BIRTH of NOAH

When 1 Enoch was first published in English, scholars noticed several passages in the Book of Parables that were inserted from another document. Some thought these were fragments of a lost Book of Noah. Although this lost book has never been discovered, there is evidence for a range of legends about Noah, some of which may appear in this section of 1 Enoch.

One of the earliest Dead Sea Scrolls, discovered in 1947, was the Genesis Apocryphon. Since its writer appears to be familiar with 1 Enoch, a date in the first century CE is possible. Although badly damaged, the scroll contains a similar story about the birth of Noah. In 1 Enoch 108, Lamech suspects the child is the result of a union with the rebellious watchers. But the Genesis Apocryphon is more explicit: Lamech believes his son is one of the Nephilim, the giants described in the Book of the Watchers. He accuses his wife, Bitenosh, of infidelity, but she swears the child is his and even recalls her pleasure on the night of Noah's conception.

The description of Noah is also similar in 1 Enoch and the Genesis Apocryphon. In both, Lamech is afraid of the infant Noah. The scroll is damaged, so the child's description is fragmentary, but his eyes shine like the sun and "this boy is flame" is close to the description in 1 Enoch.

It is likely 2 Enoch drew on the birth of Noah to describe the miraculous birth of Melchizedek. In 2 Enoch, Noah's younger brother, Nir, discovers his wife is pregnant and assumes she has been unfaithful. Although Nir kills and buries his wife, she gives birth anyway. The child is glorious in appearance and immediately dresses in priestly robes, terrifying Noah and his father. God takes young Melchizedek to Eden, where he survives the Flood.

A FINAL NOTE

In the introduction I suggested you think of this book as a tourist guidebook of 1 Enoch. Although we have come to the end of our tour, I want to encourage you to revisit your favorite places again and study them more deeply. I have included some resources at the end of this book that will guide you more deeply into the intricate world of 1 Enoch.

If you are interested in more Enoch literature, I suggest you read 2 Enoch and 3 Enoch. These books are more interested in the hierarchy of angels and the nature of eternal punishment. Reading 3 Enoch is a good first step into Jewish mysticism. If you are interested in apocalyptic books, I encourage you to read 2 Baruch or 4 Enoch, two Jewish apocalypses written at the end of the first century BCE.

RESOURCES

ONLINE

The Book of Enoch

sacred-texts.com/bib/boe/index.htm
This is the classic translation of 1 Enoch by Oxford scholar R. H. Charles. This site also has Richard Laurence's 1883 translation and Charles's Book of Jubilees.

The Enoch Seminar

enochseminar.org
A collection of scholarly resources for the study of 1 Enoch and other apocalyptic literature.

The Macedonian Conquest, Maccabees, and the Menorah

youtube.com/watch?v=0CBZgo7GXoA
A short video explaining the context and history of the Maccabean Revolt.

Old Testament Pseudepigrapha

wp.me/pjGbY-3KX
An index to my blog posts on Enoch and other apocalyptic literature.

BOOKS

The Apocalyptic Imagination: An Introduction to Jewish Apocalyptic Literature, 3rd Edition
John J. Collins, Eerdmans, 2016
Excellent overview of apocalyptic literature in early Judaism.

Introducing the Pseudepigrapha of Second Temple Judaism: Message, Context, and Significance
Daniel M. Gurtner, Baker Academic, 2020
An introduction to the literature of early Judaism, which attempts to place the books within Israel's traditions and scripture.

1 Enoch: The Hermeneia Translation
George W. E. Nickelsburg and James C. VanderKam, translators, Fortress, 2012
A modern translation of 1 Enoch based on the commentary of these noted scholars. This English translation takes into consideration all the texts now available in the Ethiopic version, the Greek texts, and the fragments from the Dead Sea Scrolls.

The Watchers in Jewish and Christian Traditions
Edited by Angela Kim Harkins, Kelley Coblentz Bautch, and John C. Endres, Fortress, 2014
A collection of scholarly essays on the watchers in Enoch and beyond.

REFERENCES

—

Ben-Dov, Jonathan. *Head of All Years: Astronomy and Calendars at Qumran in Their Ancient Context.* Leiden, Netherlands: Brill, 2008.

Boccaccini, Gabriele. *Beyond the Essene Hypothesis: The Parting of the Ways between Qumran and Enochic Judaism.* Grand Rapids, MI: Eerdmans, 1998.

Boccaccini, Gabriele, ed. *Enoch and Qumran Origins: New Light on a Forgotten Connection.* Grand Rapids, MI: Eerdmans, 2005.

Charlesworth, James H. *The Old Testament Pseudepigrapha.* New York: Doubleday, 1983.

Collins, John C., and Daniel C. Harlow, eds. *The Eerdmans Dictionary of Early Judaism.* Grand Rapids, MI: Eerdmans, 2005.

Davila, James R. "The Old Testament Pseudepigrapha as Background to the New Testament." *Expository Times* 117.2 (2005): 53–7.

Knibb, Michael. *Essays on the Book of Enoch and Other Early Jewish Texts and Traditions.* Leiden, Netherlands: Brill, 2008.

Newsom, Carol A. "The Development of *1 Enoch* 6-19: Cosmology and Judgment." *Catholic Biblical Quarterly* 42.3 (1980): 310–29.

Nickelsburg, George W. E. *1 Enoch 1: A Commentary on the Book of 1 Enoch, Chapters 1-36; 81-108.* Minneapolis, MN: Fortress, 2001.

Nickelsburg, George W. E., and James C. VanderKam. *1 Enoch 2: A Commentary on the Book of 1 Enoch, Chapters 37–82.* Minneapolis, MN: Fortress, 2011.

Portier-Young, Anathea E. *Apocalypse Against Empire: Theologies of Resistance in Early Judaism.* Grand Rapids, MI: Eerdmans, 2014.

Reed, Annette Yoshiko. *Demons, Angels, and Writing in Ancient Judaism.* New Edition. Cambridge, UK: Cambridge University Press, 2022.

Wright, Archie T. *The Origin of Evil Spirits: The Reception of Genesis 6:1–4 in Early Jewish Literature.* Minneapolis, MN: Fortress, 2015.

INDEX

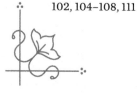

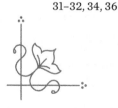

G

Gabriel, 22, 32, 34, 35, 42, 54, 61, 117
Gadreel, 79–80
Galbanum, 41
Garden of Eden, 6, 13, 20, 31, 36, 37, 39, 42, 43, 72, 75, 77, 88
Garden of Life, 75
Genesis, Book of, 2, 3, 6, 8, 13, 17, 18, 20, 30, 31, 34, 38, 41, 43, 44, 47, 56, 71, 72, 81, 87, 90, 91, 93, 100–101, 105, 111, 119
Genesis Apocryphon, 129
Geography, 29, 91, 92
Giants, 3, 13, 18, 20, 21, 25, 26–27, 28, 30
Gilgamesh, 45
Good Omens (miniseries), 32
The Good Place (TV show), 121
Great Glory, 26–27

H

Hawking, Stephen, 42
Head of Days, 63
Heaven, 43, 44, 45, 57–58, 100, 116, 121, 124–125
Heavenly tours, 29–30
Hell, 33. See also Sheol
Herodotus, 45
Hesiod, 117
Hezekiah, 31
Historical periods, 117

Holy of Holies, 77
Hume, David, 42

I

Idris, 6
Indian Ocean, 41
Isaiah, Book of, 18, 26–27, 52, 55, 60, 62, 73, 77, 88, 101, 122
Isaiah, Prophet, 15, 23, 29, 103
Ishmael, Rabbi, 2, 8
Islam, Enoch in, 6
Israel, 106, 122
It's a Wonderful Life (film), 32

J

Jacob, 119
James, Letter of, 119
Jared, 21, 81
Jason, 115
Jerusalem, 13, 25, 29, 37, 47, 90, 103, 106–107, 115
Jesus, 51, 55, 61, 62–63, 75–76, 82, 117
Job, Book of, 29, 44, 118, 124
John, Gospel of, 41, 82
John the Baptist, 55, 62
Jordan River, 105
Josephus, 28, 55
Joshua, 102, 105
Jubilees, Book of, 6–7, 8, 24, 64, 66, 90

Judah, 97, 102, 106, 116
Judaism
  angels in, 34, 77
  demons in, 28
  Enoch in, 6-7, 8
  messiah in, 51-52, 55
Jude, Book of, 2, 6, 19, 22, 36
Judges, Book of, 67, 105
Judgment Day, 15-16, 17-18,
  19, 22-23, 30, 36, 49-50,
  56, 60-63, 64, 69, 71, 120,
  123-124, 126
Justice, 60, 124

K

Kasdeya, 80
Kennedy, John F., 98
Kings, First Book of, 45
Kokabel, 21

L

Lady Wisdom, 58, 59
Lamassu, 77
Lamech, 112, 125, 128, 129
Last testaments, 111
Laurence, Richard, 4
Law of Moses, 119
Lethe (river), 31
Levi, Testament of, 38
Leviathan, 50, 69, 72, 73
Leviticus, Book of, 28

Lifestyles of the Rich and Famous
  (TV show), 37
Look Who's Talking (film), 125
Lord of Spirits, 60, 62, 63,
  74, 75-76
The Lord of the Rings
  (Tolkien), 18
Lord's Anointed One. *See* Messiah
Louis XV, 4
Luke, Gospel of, 43, 119, 127
Luminaries, Book of the, 85.
  See also Astronomical
  Writings, Book of
Lying, 82

M

Maat, 59
Maccabean Revolt, 3, 24, 97-98,
  102, 108, 112, 115-116, 117
Maccabees, Third Book of, 20
Mahalalel, 99, 101
Maps, 29, 91
Marduk, 73
Mastic, 40
Matthew, Gospel of, 18, 55, 62, 76,
  118, 120, 122, 127
Medes, 67
Melchizedek, 129
Menelaus, 115
Mesopotamian culture, 38, 42,
  45, 47, 77, 88-89, 94

Acknowledgments

Writing a short book on 1 Enoch was an adventure. I want to thank Callisto for inviting me to write this book and the editorial team, especially Adrian Potts and Beth Heidi Adelman. Beth's excellent comments made this a better book. Most of all I thank my students who have endured lectures on 1 Enoch over the years.

About the Author

 **Phillip J. Long** is a professor of biblical studies at Grace Christian University. He earned master's degrees in Biblical Exposition and Old Testament from BIOLA University and a PhD in New Testament from Andrews University. His dissertation was published as *Jesus the Bridegroom* in 2012. He published *Galatians: Freedom Through God's Grace* in 2019. He is a member of the Institute of Biblical Research and the Society of Biblical Literature.